COSMIC ISOLATION IN MUPPETS FROM SPACE

by
Michael Ray Laemmle
and
Professor Pangloss von Film-Theory

©2024 by Omega Bridge Productions
All rights reserved. No part of this book may be reproduced in any form or by any means, electronic or mechanical, including photocopying it at a Kinko's, printing it at work, or scanning it page by page and emailing the pdfs to yourself (which is simply rude).

A work such as *Muppets From Space* is a rare delight for a film analyst. Foremost among its many pleasures is that it doesn't pretend to be something it's not. It hardly has pretense to being art of any kind, and that is the very essence of its artfulness. It is, above all things, a Muppet movie, and the film is not to be understood apart from that puppet-ruled world of perpetual pranks, uninterrupted hijinks, and bottomless hilarity. From the opening credits to the last reel, a Muppet movie is always pleasantly haunted by the ghosts of a million spent chuckles. This film is no exception. We laugh, and heartily so, giggling our approval of the antics on display.

Exuding that trademark Muppet rascality, and in spades, the celluloid of this fun flick practically drips with guffaws. The quips come flying with drumbeat regularity. We discover in these sewn-together goofballs the endearing conviction that life is best thought of as an irresistible call to adventure. Even more so, the call to comical *misadventure*.

These jolly-time puppet protagonists exhibit an enviable esprit de corps. So long as they have one another, they can overcome challenges that for other comedic troupes might prove quite dire. And yet, for all the grins and gaiety we glean from Kermit and kin, this science-fiction spectacle fits into the Muppet oeuvre a bit more awkwardly than other installments in the series.

That it doesn't quite gibe with other Muppet movies should come as no surprise to the adventurer in film theory, who will quickly realize this standalone Muppet movie was contrived as an answer to the soul-sickening anxiety of a godless universe. In wrestling with the nihilism threatened by this potentially purposeless conception of the cosmos, *Muppets From Space* offers an unpretentious and candid exploration of a uniquely modern despair.

It's almost as if the unanticipated, strep-throated, septic-shock death of Jim Henson, creator of these bean-stuffed beings, forced the Muppets to reflect upon their fate as orphans set adrift in an existential void. By extrapolating from their own experience, these characters seem to have offered us some deeply earnest musings on the human condition, and even the very Death of God.

Let it be said that *Muppets From Space* is the first unflinchingly atheistic Muppet film. It posits this zany troupe of characters smack-dab in a harrowing universe, on a planet isolated from any conception of the Sacred or Eternal. These Muppets inhabit a postmodern Earth, where the historic drive toward secularism is roughly complete. The decoupling of humanity from its comforting notions of an all-knowing, all-loving deity is not up for debate, but here accepted as fact. No Muppet actually proclaims the death of God, but they needn't. History itself has made the proclamation, through the gradual momentum of civilization toward a desacralized world. General disbelief has occurred in increments, and at long last the shadow of His passing hangs over all who live.

Though there have been intellectual undercurrents in other Muppet fare, it was but thin gruel compared to the heady issues under digestion in this particular romp. The dramatic conflicts in most Muppet films remain in what we might call the sphere of the *mundane*. Political, business, and socioeconomic peccadillos are what these sewn-together thespians have been most comfortable passing commentary upon.

In a typical Muppet tale, some underhanded double-dealer wants to thwart their good-time extravaganza for ignobly materialistic reasons, and so receives a rousing comeuppance by the time we arrive at the film's last act. And while these plotlines insinuate that purely money-driven motives are deplorable, and that money-mad men and women are sociopathic in tendency, the analysis is not penetrating or of great depth.

The reluctance to dive into more controversial meat-stuff is clearly due to the Muppet grab at populist, mainstream innocuousness. These easy-going characters don't aim at provocation, oh no; their goal is *gratification*. They seek to satisfy our craving for intelligent, if not entirely philosophical, entertainments. Their art has smarts, but is by no means revolutionary or piercing.

This gentle satire is well-suited to more overtly social concerns, where the barbs of their moral wit are aimed at an easier class of villain: greedy businessmen, amoral criminals, irredeemable grumps, grouches, and sourpusses of every stripe. We empathize with the Muppets because their antagonists tend to be straw men; mere caricatures of villains; dark foils to their own good vibes and inclusive group affability. Viewers want to sing and dance with the Muppets, and are thus opposed to anyone trying to derail the hoopla.

Wanting to satisfy the audience's yen for softly scathing moral disapproval, the Muppets serve it up in light-hearted heaps.

Barely even skin deep, they shun forays into the swampy ambiguities of true critical analysis. There is no honest exploration into the social or psychological utility of such supposed vices as greed, indifference, cruelty, and hatred. Muppets advocate for the common man, and so moralize according to common prejudice.

Because their entertainments are intended for all audiences—ages one to ninety-two—their superficiality should hardly astonish us. Indeed, it is not until *Muppets From Space* that we experience a properly philosophical Muppet film, in which profundity and horseplay are given equal billing.

Though there are villains galore in *Muppets From Space*—black-suited bad guys, every one—the true enemy grappled with is the void created in the human breast when one accepts that God does not exist, and is *in absentia* from the modern world. The very malaise of contemporary life rears its thorny head here, positing our dear Muppet friends in a world devoid of the divine. In this film the dilemma is Being itself, and the absurd nature of our modern existence. The goal is hazy and unformed, the means unknown, and the enemy is everything that *is*. Our heroes appear locked in an aimless and arbitrary existence that threatens to smother all joy or sense of connection, particularly in our puppet protagonist Gonzo, the beak-nosed whatchamacallit whose spiritual plight is the primary focus of the film.

***

There may be a few cranky and quarrelsome skeptics among us, asking why a discussion of *this* work—a children's film—

instead of what is popularly regarded as an art film? Why waste time exploring *Muppets From Space*, and not, say, Bergman's *Seventh Seal*? These doubters insist that some films exist purely as an amusement, and that to look within them for deeper themes is a fool's errand, a pastime for idiots.

We adventurers in film theory know different, and insist no cultural product is unworthy of critical analysis. Indeed, we would venture one step further. It is our belief that those very films which appear most unworthy of critical scrutiny are in fact the ones most deserving of it. What goes unnoticed in a culture typically exhibits what is most deeply entrenched in that culture. Anything that stands distinctly apart as art or commentary is by necessity against the grain. Those films that slide by us undetected tell us most honestly who we really are.

For those who have eyes to see it, every creative work is a rich text begging for deconstruction. Everything that springs forth from the human mind is a signpost pointing to some higher truth. For academics, or the academically inclined, this is a truism, and as a thesis hardly needs defending. Yet there are still those among us who feel otherwise, and blissfully insist that anything not generally recognized as high art exists in a kind of context-free vacuum.

These philistines say these particular products of culture cannot yield intellectual fruit. What blindness! These fruits should be the most coveted, and when their rind is split, tasty analytical berries come spilling out as if from a cleft pomegranate. Eat up, young scholar—*feast*, ye adventurers in film theory!

Forsooth, what we might happily call "mere" art films, are too self-conscious of themselves as Art to be of much worth when addressing the Death of God. A too-great self-awareness produces self-aware art, as is wont, and art that is too conscious of itself as such lacks the natural effusion of humanity's collective unconscious flow.

All this is merely to point out why a film that naively expresses the Death of God is so essential. We adults have had to harden ourselves against the truths of modern life. This is necessary, for to not do so would be suicidal, even *contrary* to the instinct of life. But by doing so, we have sacrificed our ability to really *feel* the gut-wrenching pangs of fear brought about by God's demise.

The thoughtful adult atheist has had to incorporate his beliefs into the routine motions of responsible life. Godlessness is now but white noise buzzing at the back of his mind. To adapt, he has numbed himself to the soul-shaking implications of his ideology. The visceral response to atheism is no longer available to him. The instincts of survival warn him that, were he to follow this disagreeable notion through to its logical conclusion, he would be barred from living a sane and productive life. It would taint his entire being, from top to bottom. If God is truly dead, then life as we know it—indeed, life as we *live* it—has no obvious meaning or justification. How could we hold this truth prominently in our hearts and minds and still go on with the daily drudgery and tedium that makes up the bulk of modern life?

Ah, but certainly there was a time in his youth when this atheist buckled under from the anguish of disbelief! His knees shook, and he prayed that God would deliver the gift of faith. He tortured himself with doubts, and then again with doubts about his doubts. He plumbed the depths of his soul and mind, and was intimate with the void. He studied, poring over philosophical tomes debating the matter. He flew to the camp of Nietzsche, Marx, Darwin, and Freud. Then he swung back, feasting on the apologetics of those who would defend God's place on the throne of thrones. In the end he collapsed, and siding with his intellectual conscience, accepted that he could no longer believe. Over the years he yielded to the demands of career and family, and put aside the stormy passions of his youth. But youth is more honest, not deadened yet by experience. It still weeps and gnashes at God's passing.

A children's film, *Muppets From Space* is child-like in its handling of the Death of God, and this is what sets the film so powerfully apart from other works dealing with the same theme. The Death of God as seen through the eyes of babes. How could this not fail to strike a more powerful chord than that same Death as viewed from the perspective of some creaky old philosopher, or through the lens of some pompous old biddy of a film director?

This naiveté allows for a soulful, guttural declaration of the human condition, for which the so-called cultural mavericks and anemic creative class have not spirit nor blood enough. It is a startlingly pure expression of the uneasy angst bubbling up from our collective unconscious, revealing the troubled and profoundly ambivalent feelings we moderns have toward our own existence.

***

The youths who are now coming of age will be the first generation for which atheism is not only acceptable, but rather commonplace. Chances are good that the average child growing up in the world today will know many friends and family members who deny the existence of God. What psychological and spiritual affect this is having on the young is unknown. But we are burying our heads in the sand if we deny that the seeds of a major spiritual crisis have already been sown.

There is a gaping hole in the center of our hearts, and a cold wind howls through it. We ignore this weeping canker at our own peril. Yet truly confronting the consequences of a godless world poses a serious challenge to our sanity and wellbeing—do we have what it takes to stare into this abyss, and come away with a life-affirming spirituality?

Most of us came of age in households where religious faith still held sway. If not in our own homes, then certainly in the larger society, which has stubbornly held onto its religious sentiment. Those of us who came to reject the religious training of our youth nevertheless benefited from a firm religious ideology. It grounded us and gave us perspective, and was the glue that held our developing psyche together. Though fractured and infirm, it was a foundation upon which to build.

Due to this early ideological solidity, we have found ourselves able to nurture lives of relative normalcy. Our habits of industriousness and being socially useful beings are so ingrained in us that we can accept there is no God, no purpose, and no grand meaning to life, yet still go about our days as if little has really changed. We still follow the general trajectory towards worldly comfort and success, while at least tacitly accepting none of this rote behavior has any purpose beyond itself. Even sans God, the world still turns.

Will the generations now coming of age, and those to follow, find themselves equally able to accept the purposelessness of life and still go on living as people have these many years? Is it not likely that those who have never had the benefit of religious instruction will find, after all, that the cosmic meaningless suggested by atheism is not just unpalatable, but crushing? Will these persons, who are by no means hypothetical, find themselves oppressed by a world bereft of the hope religion provides?

When a child asks what happens to him when he dies, can we really convince ourselves that the atheistic answer will not be profoundly traumatizing to his vulnerable psyche? Even if he cannot formulate his anxiety, won't he suspect in his childish way that a world with no promise of Heaven, no hope for salvation, is a world of unspeakable horror? Are we creating toddler nihilists, whose inner light will be extinguished all too early? Will they not come to resent us for bringing them into a world so colored by hopelessness? Will they come to resent even life itself?

And what responsibility do we have as their elders and spiritual forebears to provide them with a religion that is conducive to—and informed by—the godless world they will inherit? Even if *Muppets From Space* does not provide a solution to this modern conundrum, it is at least bringing our attention to the matter. It is a warning that the issue of meaning is a far more pressing problem than many of us may suspect.

It's easy to entertain the idea that this film was created specifically to address childhood fears concerning the vast, alien, and uncompassionate universe. Like the psychological perspective on childhood displayed by other popular children's fare, it's conceivable that boatloads of demographic studies were undertaken to find out what today's children truly fear. This is entirely hypothetical, and I have no idea what such studies might reveal. But I do know that we tend to tell ourselves children are ignorant of these higher philosophical matters. We believe their biggest fears are monsters under the bed and being alone in the dark. Could we be deceiving ourselves?

I myself was very young when I became a religious skeptic. I became increasingly convinced that the religious indoctrination I suffered was an edifice of lies. I had nowhere to turn. The God I was told to worship seemed more like a demonic villain than a merciful creator. This kind judge would remorselessly condemn me to an eternity of torment for a litany of sins. Beyond petty, this God was vengeful and pitiless to an infinite degree. What a horrific way to understand reality!

Simultaneously, I was encouraged to despise others for believing differently, for entertaining different moralities, and for indulging in behaviors that were irrationally taboo. I was force-fed a creation story and historical account that was clearly mythological, and told it was evil to doubt its hard factuality. In deference to the secular world, I was encouraged to use my mind as a tool for critical thinking—but when it came to religion, I was warned against analytical thought, under threat of consequences that were profoundly terrifying.

More troubling than the factual inaccuracies of religion, a morality that was clearly detrimental to the human spirit was heaped on me. It was obvious this religion was born of pure hatred, but couched in glowing terms of love and universal brotherhood. It wouldn't be until I was in my early twenties that I came across a lucid account of how this religion of hate convinced itself of its good and loving intentions. I found this in the works of Nietzsche, whose ideas are wrestled with in every frame of *Muppets From Space*, as we shall see.

Until then, I had only a half-formed idea of the psychological acrobatics necessary to believe in Christianity. I only had an instinctual aversion to its insidious ability to warp the minds and hearts of its adherents. To paraphrase Nietzsche, my disbelief in Christianity came not to be about *reasons*, but about good taste.

Even if I had discovered Nietzsche earlier, I would have had no one to whom I could express my growing distaste for religion. I was surrounded by hypocrites who tailored these allegedly sacrosanct tenets to suit their lives, ignoring all those they had no personal interest in abiding by. If called to account they became angry, and would go to great lengths to rationalize their noncompliance. All the while they nurtured a hatred for those who did the same as they did, the only difference between them being the tenets ignored.

Jesus said judge not, lest ye be judged—but judgment, accusation, and self-righteousness were built into the very creed of Christianity itself. How could all these people I knew and loved—my very community—adhere to this ceremonial rubbish? That normal, otherwise healthy adults could hold this religion true was far more terrifying than vampires, werewolves, and bogeymen.

Searching for answers, I buried myself in books of popular science. I eagerly read up on physics, anthropology, history, biology, and geology. I was seduced by the clarity of thought, argumentation from evidence, and the openness to new facts and interpretations. It was a brave new world, and I allied myself with these articulate and educated rationalists.

The trouble was that science pointed towards nothing but a nihilistic view of humanity. Our origins, eventual fate, insignificance in the universe, and our painfully brief existence as a species, all led to some troubling conclusions about what it actually meant to be a human being. The truth about our kind was so disturbing! I could hardly agree with the likes of Carl Sagan and his ilk, who naively promised that the romance of scientific investigation could somehow stand in for the comforting falsehoods provided by religion.

I doubt that my intellectual development was much different than other children my age. And certainly nowadays, when scientific knowledge—and knowledge of every kind—is much easier to access via Internet and popular television programs, there is an entire generation that will have to struggle in the same way I did. Having had conversations with parents about this issue, I sense that I'm not far off. Our parents and grandparents, when asked difficult questions about the meaning of life, felt obliged to tell a comforting lie.

Parents today are more inclined to be intellectually honest with their offspring. When asked what the meaning of life is, they freely admit they do not know. That the well of lies has gone dry may prove a positive development, but it's worrisome that we don't yet have the words to dampen the dread our children feel regarding our kind's cosmic isolation. We cannot stomach lies, we cannot stomach truths. We are fractured and uncertain.

When the childhood nightmares are of this existential kind, a parent cannot simply run a flashlight under the bed or into the corners of the closet and declare the entire world a safe-zone. No, this bogeyman called the Modern Paradigm is everywhere and nowhere; it is the air we breathe. It seeps into our souls like black tar.

Certainly the issue of youthful existential dread must be addressed, for as astronomical and scientific education becomes more widespread, we will not long hereafter have a generation whose deepest philosophical concerns about the Earth's place in the scheme of existence are not being adequately addressed by the culture at large.

This inadequacy will leave children susceptible to the idiotic fancies and pseudo-beliefs of charlatans, shamans, new-agers, and drug-addled demagogues of every stripe. In this way *Muppets From Space* fills a social and cultural niche, the importance of which lay far beyond the confines of cinematic entertainment. Indeed, it may one day prove a spiritual manual for pre-adolescents concerned about humanity's tottering over a precipice of annihilation and doom. Anxiety of this soul-penetrating kind will no doubt be the hallmark emotional state of children in the coming decades, and they will require art that acknowledges this.

What is more, films like this are helpful in aiding the adult who has retained his youthful fancy that human beings hold some grand significance within the scheme of things. This may prove true in the future, based upon data we could scarcely imagine in our present day. But for now it proves to be an immature conception of the world, and what is worse, a stumbling block to our higher destiny. Our destiny is to weather the spiritual, psychological, and social storms created by what should now be considered a historical event, the Death of God. A post-theistic society is painfully being born, and is probably a historical eventuality. But such a birth still needs midwives.

***

Did the filmmakers know what they were doing when they crafted this masterwork of psychological angst? Did they even hear faintly the symphony they were themselves composing? Could this kind of naiveté, these innocent effusions, be externally imposed, consciously constructed, and carefully controlled? I say not. These filmmakers went into this project trying to make a mere Muppet Movie—a caper, an adventure, a rollicking romp—and only accidentally produced a modern masterpiece of religious brooding.

In fact, Frank Oz, a major player on the film, said *Muppets From Space* was not the film they wanted, nor intended it to be. This itself is telling. The makers of the film knew not what they had done—and we are the better for it. If they'd set out to consciously create a film dealing with this contemporary angst, it surely would have been a botch; too calculated, too artificial, too tinkered with.

The underlying insinuation encoded in the film is that we are, all of us, heirs to a darker conception of life than any prior generation has known. Lurking in the shadowy blur of our daily goings-on is a truth we are fiercely hesitant to face: that ours is an empty existence, with no justification beyond itself. Our aims have no lasting resonance, so we look within ourselves for the justification we cannot find externally. But having been conditioned to seek the meaning of life outside ourselves—in God, in our social world—we come to see that we are unprepared for this immense shift to an egocentric conception of our lives. Deprived of the spiritual tools to impose our own meaning on the world, we struggle to find lasting wholeness.

When there is no eternity for our deeds to reverberate through, our actions begin to feel stillborn, and lack gravity. No good or ill we do, nothing of what we build and strive for, holds meaning when stacked against the ocean of time in which we so briefly swim. What are we building towards? What is our motivation? As the presence of God ebbs, we strive to seek a meaning within ourselves. Like Narcissus, we become utterly self-interested in a doomed effort to find wholeness in the modern world.

Or perhaps we look to our fellow human beings for the source of contentment we've been deprived of. However, our worldly companions offer no sure substitute. Placing our hopes for eternal meaning in finite beings—which we are—is an easily recognizable folly, and leads to disappointment and despair. With nowhere to turn, our spiritual needs become as urgent as they are impossible to satisfy. Our very finiteness is what most offends our sensibilities, and we wish to have the purpose for our being nestled in the bosom of some higher power.

It has been hypothesized that among the social and psychological uses of God is that such a belief connects us to the eternal. If there is no everlasting being to keep record of our existence, than the brief blip that is our meager portion of years becomes insufferable, for in that case even our grandest deeds become the flailing gestures of gnats. The human mind is hopeful, and we would have our deeds echo through the halls of eternity.

This feeling that what we do we here has significance in the sway of history can motivate us to great deeds, and without it we expose ourselves to the risk of nihilism and the dilemma of doubt. This doubt is insidious, and taints not only our day-to-day decisions, but the entire world, from top to bottom. It blackens everything until many of us can no longer find even a modicum of joy in the varied offerings of life.

Many students of history understand the entire movement into the modern world as a centuries-long struggle from out the shadow of God. Religious belief, entrenched in our own psyches and permeating society at every level, came to be increasingly seen as delusional, and unquestionably harmful to humanity's own self-interest. Religious squabbles had been the spur to many devastating wars, but the destructiveness of religion was thought to extend far beyond this.

These horrid superstitions, having arisen from the minds of ignorant, illiterate, and primitive peoples, had been passed down through the ages and over time literally corrupted everything. All of our social institutions were stained with a lie. Even more tragic and damaging was the affect these beliefs had on the individual, who suffered from these cruel and effacing doctrines as if from a terminal disease.

Belief was seen as an affront to human dignity, and a prison for the mind. Priests and holy men were considered charlatans who made use of religious precepts and structures to gain power and manipulate an ignorant and bedazzled populace. The very concept of God as we were given to understand Him was attacked as ridiculous and contradictory.

A supreme being who constructed the entire cosmos simply for our benefit? A tyrant who could see into our most private thoughts and feelings, and judge them as either to His liking or not? A supposedly loving creator who would nevertheless condemn us to eternal torment for minor infractions and insults to His vanity? None of this made any sense whatsoever, and the times were such that critics of religion could express their radical views with a reasonable amount of openness.

To these atheists, disbelief seemed to promise a kind of Golden Age. The moment one personally stopped believing in God was like breaking the chains of bondage. Subservience to irrationality and theological injustice was no more. A kind of exhilaration swept over these infidels. They staggered at the possibilities now open to them, and the freedom of thought they would now be allowed. And so elated with these new vistas—the fresh, clean air they now breathed—these pioneers pondered over the enormous benefits civilization itself might gain if religion was discarded. It was assumed humanity as a whole would experience the same deep gladdening of the spirit when it too shrugged off the burden of faith and the beguiling notion of sin.

Through the application of reason and careful methodology, it was thought that a utopia could be built—a society where men and women lived full and purposeful lives, with every opportunity to maximize their human potential. It was believed this would be more than enough to make life meaningful for the average person. What more could people want than to be free of superstition, and to think and do as one saw fit, all according to a rational code of ethics?

These irreligious thinkers—not all of them atheists, to be sure—did indeed shape the civilization of today. Through their secular humanist writings they attacked established religious, political, and social customs. They laid the groundwork for contemporary forms of democracy, human rights, and economic organization; all held together by reason and the rule of law, enshrined forever in written constitutions. They forced the decoupling of religion from politics, and through the influence of their doctrines helped found the world's modern secular societies.

Religious thought was certainly not vanquished, as the more radical among them would have preferred. And though it appears to many that religiosity is thriving within most societies, especially the United States, this would perhaps be to claim too much. For all the pockets of a thriving personal and group religion, the actual world we inhabit runs on its own secular terms.

The concept of God has been so diminished and dethroned that today when we speak of Him we are making reference to a much more wispier and airless being than the generations of faithful who have come before us. And every year this concept of God gets thinner and more bloodless, until one day, doubtless, it will vanish altogether—poof, like a snuffed out candle.

Today we understand that secular thinkers were naïve concerning human adaptability to an irreligious world. Mankind may never be capable of calling such a world home; the religious need seemingly forever embedded in our kind. As a species we have collectively set up institutions whereby our physical needs are met. This of course applies foremost to those of us lucky enough to have been born into wealthier nations. But with obvious exceptions, the great majority of us are able to procure adequate shelter, nutrition, and all the basics of modern comfort and convenience.

This has introduced an ironic twist, in that by being so freed we are vulnerable to needs of a more pressing kind. That we find solutions to this predicament is essential, because there may well come a time in our future when the majority lives with health, but finds that suddenly, having procured the means of living, they have no reason to live. It is a religious craving that we have, though we are no longer religious.

Atheism and agnosticism are the two fastest growing spiritual orientations in the United States. Almost 25% of our citizenry claims no religious affiliation. Priests, pastors, rabbis and their ilk are daily to be found reciting anecdotes alleged to illustrate the consequences of faithlessness. Sensational acts of violence, rape, apathy, selfishness, and the moral drift of young and old alike are seen as consequences of God's removal from the public sphere and moral discourse. A student shoots up his school, and the pundits of holiness cite the removal of prayer from school. Venereal disease is on the rise. The institution of marriage is in irreversible decay. Substance abuse is rampant. All of this attributable, we are told, to the shouldering of God from out of our hearts.

Though it's difficult to endorse these agitated histrionics, it would be remiss to say there is no truth whatsoever in these claims. For millennia, God has acted as a lodestone, guiding us along through our days. Without this guide, a sense of broad purposelessness has taken root, and this waywardness is a sign of the pervasive nihilism. Humanity has not yet been able to posit or universally impose a unifying goal that compensates for the loss of our theistic ideological structure. Life is hard and full of anguish.

As Nietzsche pointed out, mankind is able to endure an immense amount of suffering, so long as he believes it has meaning. While the meaning has been lost, the suffering remains, so we cast about desperately for an explanation to our plight, an answer to the question, *Why?*, and beg deliverance from a God who no longer exists.

We must remember that a general atheism is a recent trend. It has only been a decade or two that nonbelievers have felt comfortable expressing their thoughts on religious faith in public. And even though atheists are accorded a voice in the marketplace of ideas, they remain to some degree pariahs. Politicians are still wary of publicly committing to atheism for fear their constituencies will rebel against them. Aspersions are cast on unbelievers, and they are thought to be less moral and trustworthy than those who profess religious faith.

This is in spite of studies that show the non-religious are as moral, or even more so, than their religious counterparts. The world still fears the atheist and his message, so much so that atheism is literally outlawed in many nations, and in some places the penalty for unbelief is imprisonment and death. Among us Westerners, a professed atheism will more than likely draw sneers, disapproval, pity, and misunderstanding.

And though the atheist is likely to decry this state of affairs, it's worth pointing out that the shroud of godlessness blanketing modern civilization may have far-reaching ramifications that were never intended or foreseen—not all of them cheery or encouraging.

The many vocal atheists among us today tend to be of a rather optimistic strain. They just seem to know the world will be vastly improved when religion is discarded as a crippling holdover from our eons of ignorance. But is such optimism justified? Has it ever been? Would an absence of superstition be beneficial to humanity? What else do we stand to lose when we lose our God?

As the famed German philosopher Friedrich Nietzsche was wont to point out, sometimes lies are far more beneficial than truths. The truth can be harmful, even *antithetical* to life. And an enormous deception may be necessary for creatures like us to go on, to do it all again for one more day, to endure.

If we don't experience truth as a danger, we are probably not really experiencing truth. For what truth do we turn to when religious truth has been so besieged, belittled, and attacked? We turn to science, as if knowledge alone could secure the existential comfort we require. But scientific knowledge has belittled humanity. It has confirmed our smallness, our precariousness, and our inconsequential relationship to reality as a whole.

The danger godlessness poses to humanity doesn't lay especially in the moral realm, as most believers tend to think. Without fear of God restraining us, it's unlikely that society will become a Bacchanalia of violence, sex, and rampant immorality. The world without God as a place where "all is permitted" is a paranoid fantasy. Morality grows out of our evolutionary history as social beings. Codified religious ethics are only a post-rationalization of sorts, and generally unconvincing at that.

Without faith our moral landscape would probably remain more or less as it is. Our social instincts are the true bedrock of conscience, as is our reliance on others for security and happiness. It takes a rather morbid, and probably ignorant, conception of the human being to suppose that without religion we would transform into sociopathic monsters. If not in the moral realm, then what exactly is the threat posed to us by godlessness?

Nietzsche famously expressed this troubling reality in a short story in his book, *The Joyful Science.* In what is called *The Parable of the Madman*, a rather anxious gentleman takes up his lantern in the wee hours of dawn and thrusts himself into a square to desperately beg of God's whereabouts. *I seek God, I seek God*, he cries. Many atheists were in the square just then, and they overheard him (apparently atheists liked to gather there).

They laughed at the madman's hysterics, mocking the very premise of his question. But in a burst of potent eloquence, the madman challenges the atheists to see the true magnitude of what they have done, to recognize the consequences of atheism, of in fact being the murderers of God. Without God, mankind's entire world becomes unhinged. Everything—from morality to meaning—has been undone. The Earth is unmoored, adrift on uncertain seas.

We are, all of us, Gonzo.

***

It is fitting that we dive into our exploration of the film by first examining its promotional poster. Even the most dabbling of analysts knows promotional materials are created not so much to convey the heart and soul of a film, but often enough to misrepresent it entirely. The more a film is at odds with audience expectations of it, the more it will have to cloak its true self.

Muppets From Space is a textbook example of the phenomena, and the promotions can kindly be described as bait-and-switch advertising. This is hardly meant as criticism. Marketers do what they must to get bodies into theaters, and it would hardly have been feasible, from an advertising perspective, to promote the film in fealty to its true nature.

What mainstream critics and audiences expect of a Muppet movie is only tangentially on display in the film. And yet for all that, it is a Muppet movie and must be sold as such. These puppets dance and twirl and jest, regardless of the grim backdrop to their merry-making. In fact, buffoonery and mirth are advocated as the very antidotes to the wretched poison of modern melancholy.

This corrective to despair has historical precedent. As the saying goes, "Eat, drink, and be merry—for tomorrow we die." More than just a reminder of our mortality or a call to celebration, this old chestnut affirms the use of merriment as a weapon against nihilism. Gloom is a dark cavern, and laughter echoing off its walls acts as a lantern. Jokes and joy can be worn like armor. Chuckle on, dear friends—heave off your glumness.

Yet the reeking fumes of despair the film emits are not necessarily shooed by the strenuous fanning of our giggles. Quite the opposite. It is said that even in laughter the heart will sorrow, and the end of mirth is grief. The dank stench of sadness in the film is actually stirred up by the hee-hawing, conjured into the air as if by some sniggering séance.

This overpowering bouquet of dashed hopes wafts upward through our nostrils, the mainlines to the mind, and we howl like gleeful lunatics who have peered long into the abyss. This blast of equal parts humor and heartache is a juxtaposition, but never a jarring one. Levity and heaviness of soul are so intimately entwined that we experience both feelings simultaneously, as one merged emotion.

More profound than the mere idea of laughter as antidote to despair—but in some ways related to it—Nietzsche endorsed a Dionysian approach to modernity. Dionysus was the Greek god of intoxication, associated with drunkenness, dancing, music, and the affirmation of life through ecstatic experience. Though existence may be a tragic spectacle, it must be affirmed as a good, and not just in spite of its painful elements.

Suffering and joy are to be embraced simultaneously, as both are inseparable components of sentient existence. We achieve the most blessed state of euphoria when affirming the whole of life, good and bad. This is the great Yes! to life Nietzsche speaks of. Music is a lubricant to this transcendence, and *Muppets From Space* utilizes the genre that today most readily gets our bodies moving and booties shaking: funk (which we will discuss in a later chapter).

Fittingly then, on the poster in question we are graced with a UFO landing pod populated by some of the most seminal Muppet personalities, along with a few friends newly introduced to the pantheon. Everyone in the pod shines with an open-jawed grin stretching ear to ear, as if they've all just pulled their heads from a drum of laughing gas.

Dizzied with elation, these camera-ready Muppets must surely see life as hilarious to an almost infinite degree. Even soul-sick Gonzo—donned in his tinfoil tuxedo—has his arms upraised, as if coming off the adrenaline high of some exhilarating victory. The poster screams nothing but "romp." *Come see this lighthearted and life-affirming escapade, ye happy-go-lucky filmgoers!*

Ruminating over initial responses to the film, it becomes abundantly clear that nobody really knew what movie it was they'd just seen. As often happens with forward-looking works of art, there was no context by which to consider it. Even to this day there hardly exists an analyst who sees *Muppets From Space* for the anguished meditation it is. The reactions of media acolytes who reviewed it during its theatrical release were especially telling. Not one critic addressed the philosophical matters displayed front and center, and only one or two even made mention of the film's dark overtones. One writer suggested the material might be too grim for young children. That the subject might be too grim for any living being seems not to have crossed her mind. There is nowhere even the hint of suspicion that the film's entire purpose was to expose the fissure beneath our very feet, slowly yawning into a chasm.

This is not to blame our dear critics, who are mostly vested in letting moviegoers know what satisfies the base requisite need for escapism in an upcoming weekend. No reasonable person would expect a film of great despondency and depth to come from the realm of Muppetry. Everyone was blindsided. Whereas most went into theaters expecting good old-fashioned family entertainment, catchy songs, and a wealth of good gag jokes, *Muppets From Space* is one of the bleakest films ever committed to celluloid. The film's jokes, gibbering, and guffaw-inducing pratfalls only serve to put the melancholia of the film in starker relief. In this sense maybe the posters weren't far off, advancing the proposition that viewers would chuckle like unhinged madmen at the reflection of their own tortured souls.

The tagline on the *Muppets From Space* movie provides a key to the entire Muppet response to spiritual crisis. It reads as follows: "SPACE: IT'S NOT AS DEEP AS YOU THINK." Of course the tagline is a sly and self-deprecating announcement of what may be called the air of zaniness throughout the film. No doubt there is a certain shallowness in the Muppetistic response to humanity's existential crisis, and it is even played for laughs. But shallowness should not necessarily be thought of as the incorrect response to our irresolvable plight.

Indeed, to avoid becoming morose and ineffectual as human beings, it is a certain lightness in the loafers that will keep us able to bear our condition through to the unforeseen end. When we become deep, all-too deep, it may signal to us that we are sinking into a glum morass. Far better to pull yourself from this bog, and skip lightly across the dreary moor.

However, because I am not here to promote the film as a laugh-a-minute spectacle, I can freely suggest a more descriptive and honest tagline, this one for the more contemplative moviegoer: "SPACE: THERE IS NOTHING TO FEAR FROM ITS UNUTTERABLE VASTNESS AND GODLESSNESS."

In the final analysis, the film attempts to remain optimistic, if not about our fate, then our ability to accept and overcome it. Whether that optimism is justified, or whether the film succeeds in neutralizing its somber insinuations, is for the individual viewer to decide. But we as a species probably do have the psychological and spiritual resources to accept the dismal truth about ourselves and move on. At least, it's pretty to think so.

Hope springs eternal in the human breast. We may one day emerge from our current state of impotent doubt to a higher plane, concocting spiritual responses adequate to a godless existence. As yet, we struggle to build a general paradigm through which to comprehend the world. Individual philosophers and theologians have certainly presented options to the world, but as yet none have widely taken root. Perspectives on how life is to be understood and lived remain idiosyncratic and fragmented.

Condemned to individuality and freedom of personal choice, we cultivate viewpoints that are appropriate only for us, and shared with nobody. But a paradigm that is not generally shared is not a paradigm at all, but rather a nook from which to view the world. Each one of us is a lone wanderer, devising our own moralities. These can only fail to satisfy, because we are a social species, uncomfortable with isolation and hungry for connection.

By adhering to strictly personal spiritual paradigms we may attain a sense of that nobility accorded the lone wolf, but risk disappearing into the rabbit holes of our own mind, and thereby grow aloof and alienated from the outer world. This solipsistic existence is its own singular brand of damnation. It turns each one of us into a detached shard, incapable of communicating our deepest thoughts and musings to others. Like a cosmonaut confined within the walls of his one-man pod, drifting off into deep space, we either succumb to madness or numb ourselves in an effort to preserve sanity.

Humans have so far demonstrated a knack for unlimited psychological adaptation. We have elastic minds. Profound ideological shifts have occurred continuously throughout our hundred thousand years or so as a species; and here we still are, getting up in the morning and making it through the day. Old gods die, and buried along with them the all-encompassing explanations of the universe they were representatives of. But today revolutions happen within spans of a few years, months, or even days. Technology, media, and new scientific knowledge alter our sense of reality with startling regularity.

What was accepted as truth just yesterday might tomorrow be proven false. Those of us concerned with intellectual clarity, and equipped with a desire to know the world as it is, are driven daily to assimilate new knowledge and alter our conception of the world accordingly. Unable to keep pace with the accumulation of knowledge, we are forced to hold ourselves in a kind of suspension of belief, unwilling to accept even the most commonly held assumptions as fact.

We swim in an ocean of skepticism and suspicion. Doubt becomes the very air we breathe, infusing us through to the deepest marrow.

Even so, it has been claimed by more luminous minds than mine that the paradigm shifts of the last few hundred years have still not been digested by the larger population. Relativity, evolution, moral relativism, and the like are so disagreeable to the human constitution that we cannot break the revelations down and assimilate them into our systems. There are even those who claim we haven't truly accepted—deep down into our bones—the displacement of the Earth from the center of the universe, or even the heliocentric view of the solar system. Mentally and spiritually, we prefer ancient presumptions over contemporary reality, which is often counterintuitive and difficult to grasp.

Generally speaking, ideology arises from social organization, not the other way around. New ideas regarding the human condition arise when socioeconomic conditions suggest them. Known as cultural lag, this phenomenon means society at large tends to be a few steps behind the times, until the zeitgeist settles over all or most of a people like a fine dust. Today we deal with a problem no prior civilization has had to grapple with. Paradigm shifts of old took effect at a pace which seems absolutely glacial in comparison to the speed of modern life. Technology sprints breathlessly ahead of us, and we strive to catch up. Our social world is upended almost daily, and we embrace these changes while simultaneously struggling to comprehend their implications. Today, we must be faster, stronger, and smarter than any generation that has come before us if we are to forge a spiritual adaptation. The race goes to the swift, but are we speedy enough?

At the same time our spiritual needs have become more urgent, our options for material comfort have expanded beyond any one person's ability to indulge them. We're becoming soft around the middle—and may lack the force of will necessary to the task at hand. We enjoy countless distractions in all forms of media: video games, movies, books, television, and the choice offerings of the Internet. Life-affirming hobbies abound, and are a siren call to a life of seemingly infinite leisure: rock-climbing, yoga, journaling, cycling, swimming, Pilates, and weekend obstacle courses.

Meanwhile, humanity is exposed to practical threats from every direction. Global war may seem implausible to us, but the last one was a mere two generations ago. We are still multiplying like rabbits, and technological advances in food and energy production are unlikely to keep pace with need. Some super virus could wipe us out. An asteroid is surely headed right for us as we speak, and will wipe our species from the planet when it strikes.

All these challenges, and now with the suspicion—for many an unquestionable certainty—that we alone shoulder the responsibility of sorting out our affairs, and cannot rely on cosmic guidance or divine wisdom. There is no God with a plan, no fate, and no end game. It's a troubling reality, to say the least. The human of today must will the human of the future, and find a way, a direct path, to a goal that for now remains ambiguous. *Muppets From Space* is merely a signpost, a giant X on a map. It tells us where we are at the moment, and how far we've come. But it also shows us how much farther still have to go. And we still have miles to go.

We still have miles to go.

***

As is apt, *Muppets From Space* begins with a rolling image reminding us of the true physical vastness of the universe. Stars fly rapidly by until they blur into streaming white lines, the light-years that separate them compressed into one luminous mesh. Yet even at the speed of light—Captain Kirk's beloved warp speed—one could never travel so fast as to blur the very stars. This cosmos is an enormity utterly beyond the scope of humanity's finite mind to process.

We often make a game of trying to bring these distances closer to home, putting them in familiar terms that do nothing but provide the illusion of understanding. We find incomparable joy in likening the Earth to a basketball, and the moon to a tennis ball placed a few yards away—and so on. This children's game entertains us, to be sure. It even comforts us. We foolishly convince ourselves these flimsy metaphors put the measureless universe within our grasp.

All this colorful word play is mere verbal ploy and deception. Even our own solar system is tremendously beyond our scale of comprehension. And the familiar star system we call home is but one of billions, a far-flung suburb of our indistinct galaxy, itself one of billions of other galaxies of similar stature. Our meagerness alone is enough to destroy the spirit in many of our breasts. How can we even begin to feel at home in a physical reality whose very magnitude is so astonishing?

We stretch our imaginations to breakage when trying to envision the great sea of nothingness that is space, but still often fail to apprehend our measly place within it. This infinite smallness becomes the most convincing argument for our personal meaninglessness. It is much more persuasive than any philosophical ramble. How could we possibly enjoy any transcendent purpose, standing as we do in such painfully diminished scale to the whole of creation? We are motes of dust on a pebble. We stare into the night sky and tremble.

Perhaps you are one of those joyful souls who imagines us living on another planet, orbiting a different sun, in a solar system far better and more enlightened than our own? Friends, this is fantasy and delusion. We will not be living on Pluto, Saturn, Mars, or any other giant stone in the galaxy. We are going to die here, us and everybody else; the dogs and the cats and the deer, the alligators and the jellyfish.

And yes, Virginia, even the whales and spotted owls. I'm loathe to spoil the ending, but one day we will all of us go the way of the dinosaurs, and become losers at the game of Life. When extinction comes—and it will come—we will have been but a blip in the radar, fading into obscurity like drops of water in the ocean deep.

How big is the universe? Traveling at a mind-boggling speed of 42,000 miles per hour, the space probe Voyager 2 still took twelve years to reach Neptune, the planet furthest from the Earth. With gravitationally assisted propulsion, at this time the most feasible technology, we're still burdened with 76,000 years to reach Proxima Centauri, the nearest star. This means roughly 2,600 human generations.

To put this in perspective, let's ask what we ourselves were up to this many generations back. There were only around ten thousand human beings, and we passed our time hunting and gathering on the savannahs of Africa. Nobody had yet made the long journey north into southern Europe. Around ten thousand years ago, a mere *tenth* of the time the journey to our neighboring star would take, humans invented agriculture. Time and distance are eternal enemies in this regard.

What this reality does is plant us firmly on Earth, crucified to the pale blue marble. As a maturing species, we must rid ourselves of the childish hope that we can defer a reckoning by pushing ourselves further out into space. Even if colonization of distant planets were a practical reality, our spiritual crisis would by no means become less pressing—it will follow us wherever we might roam.

An inheritance from our frontier mythology, it is a distinctly American ambition to escape ourselves by pushing further out into the hinterlands. In the wilds of what was then the untamed western border of the nation, pioneers were able to abandon the constraints of civilization, discovering the freedom to create themselves according to their own wills. We cling to this frontier mythology, but new climes no longer have the power to provide this freedom. The frontier is closed, and we must point our compasses inward. We must travel into inner space, and form ourselves anew from whatever strange materials we find.

Fantastically then, the beginning of *Muppets From Space* puts us in the perspective of some being or entity for whom the vastness of space is no obstacle to mobility. It's rational to assume we are seeing the Earthbound approach of Gonzo's alien kin, through their own eyes. They zip through space with some clear intent upon our planet.

Having just dismissed this kind of traverse through the cosmos as impossible (or nearly enough so), we can still eagerly acknowledge that these early scenes burst with flavorful thematic juices, able to sate the thirst of even the most demanding analysts. Drink up, I dare say—these hearty thematic juices are of a tasty, quaffable sort.

Here we are presented with what is at least a theoretically possible account of space travel—worm holes. Intergalactic tunnels are being utilized as shortcuts through the space-time continuum. As in other films, this theoretical postulation is being used to imaginarily close the distances between celestial bodies. This is a subtle but necessary inclusion, for if the film were not based somehow in scientific plausibility, no matter how farfetched, we could all of us take its philosophical musings a bit less seriously.

This is a trope quite common in science fiction films, so that we see some kind of scientific rationale for an irrational premise. But what's important to remember is that this film is not primarily science fiction, but rather a philosophical and spiritual one. So why would a film demonstrate such eagerness for grounding in at least hypothetical science—here, at the beginning—when throughout the rest of the film scientific plausibility is sacrificed to surrealistic fantasy time and again?

Clearly, because we are to understand that the spiritual melancholy portrayed in the film is a result of scientific knowledge itself.

Science has given us a great deal to chew on. Verily, it has diminished us completely. Many popular advocates of science—from Carl Sagan to Richard Dawkins—believe the scientific search for knowledge offers enough romantic allure to displace the nihilism inherent in its conclusions. This may be true for those individual seekers professionally vested in the sciences, but for the layman this knowledge is cold comfort.

Science has left man dwindling, and with every discovery further depreciated his worth. Yes, we drop our jaws at the complexity we find in nature, and particularly in ourselves. But it seems to us this complexity has stacked upon itself without aim or inclination. Not blindly, no, for we have evolved as vehicles for the expression of our genetic code. But this miserly aim hardly satisfies our needs as sentient beings.

What rosy pictures does science paint for us? The Earth is but a grain of dust in this dreadfully overwhelming cosmos. As a species we can still hardly believe it, much less accept it, though it has been a numbing certainty for nearly four hundred years. We stand in awe of the incomprehensible vastness, and though it is an intangible thing—a concept—we feel this vastness gnawing away at our wellbeing and at our sanity.

Our very souls shudder at the nothingness we stand upon, and the thin ice our entire existence is built over. As beings we are thinner than ghosts, and our entire history, our entire conception of ourselves as a species, is just as transparent and vaporous. This Milky Way, a fine galaxy to us perhaps, is one among untold billions. How can we not weep for our lonesome and isolated selves?

We are precariously balanced in orbit around a ticking time bomb of a star. We will most assuredly die before this sun goes supernova—but if by some miracle we still find ourselves alive on this planet some millions of years down the road, we will be nicely incinerated when the bright ball goes kaboom. We float adrift in formless ether, vulnerable to solar flares, asteroids, and other cosmic death-dealers. We are alive by the privilege of chance and nothing more.

And vis-à-vis this reality, it is not death that carries the most worrisome sting. It is living consciousness that is most agonizing. For we the living are burdened with a clear look into the abyss of meaninglessness that characterizes our lives above all other characterizations. And on the Earth itself, humankind is but one of what may as well be an infinite number of species, each with especial claims to distinction, each with equal chances of escaping its eventual fate. In the world presented to us by science and rational analysis, our end is doom. The fruits of civilization are miraculous, to be sure, but no less masturbatory for that.

That humanity has not utterly incorporated or digested this view should not be surprising, nor should it necessarily be taken as a sign of weakness or ignorance. In fact it could imply several things. It might even be a sign of the greatest strength and self-knowledge. Humanity as a monolithic and undifferentiated entity is quite rightly cautious about accepting any doctrine that would place its own inherent value and right to exist in question. For was it by doubting our right to existence that we rose to the top of the food chain? But the implications of science remain clear. Though we favor ourselves as quite special, this only betrays our bias towards ourselves.

Being a great admirer of the scientific endeavor, I can and do sympathize with the scientist who slaps his forehead in response to statistics that reveal the average American's disregard for scientific opinion, and for what in the world of science are accepted truths. What well-established tenets of scientific thought will the public not casually dismiss next? There is disbelief in even the most basic mechanics of Darwinian evolution, and scientific advisors are conveniently ignored when need be. However, I would console and comfort our dear scientist with a suggestion.

Were humanity as a whole to adopt a cosmic paradigm which compacts itself into a meaningless collection of biochemical processes on a planet of no particular significance, in a galaxy of very little distinction, we would be forced into the desolate wilderness of utter nihilism. This nihilism, if truly felt, would lead to social circumstances for which science, political progress, or indeed such superfluous activities as filmmaking, would be an impossibility. Carnality would be the daily leaven for every individual on the planet.

Science gives us no reason to believe in ourselves, which is why Nietzsche called it out as the very midwife of modern nihilism. There may be nobility in persevering under the shadow of a grisly truth, but lies and ignorance of the facts may be the only barriers keeping the ravages of truth at bay.

The existence of wormholes, by closing the distance between points in the universe, neutralizes to some degree the terrors of space, even as it seems to make us vulnerable to others. For example, the existence and utility of wormholes could conceivably lead to an unwelcome visitation from hostile and near-blasphemous creatures who intend only to agonize us with physical and mental tortures.

The film thus acknowledges the danger of wormholes, but insists that as long as we are weaving myths about the cosmos, we may as well weave joyful ones. Generally speaking, in times of uncertainty the healthy instinct sides with notions that *affirm* life. Our vulnerability is here posited as an opportunity for deeper knowledge and understanding of reality, with at least the chance that such understanding can lead to a hopeful outcome.

It's worth noting here that a debate currently rages among astronomers about whether or not we should really be attempting to make contact with alien races. Most famously, cosmologist Stephen Hawking has spoken out against attempting to make this kind of interstellar connection. His concern, as ours should be, is that an alien civilization is as likely, if not more so, to be hostile.

Like all civilizations, they will be in need of the natural resources that abound on our planet. Why should we assume their primary interest will not be to conquer and enslave us, and rape our planet of its material wealth? Hawking cites the New World's discovery of the Old, and how devastating that was for the native peoples of North and South America. We may fare equally poorly when aliens alight on our own terrestrial sphere.

This introduces an interesting debate about an open versus a closed world. In part, the eagerness for contact with alien races reflects a desire to look outside ourselves for answers to the many conundrums we face. Presumably aliens would have some insight on how to survive the rocky transition into a technological civilization. To advocate that we close ourselves off to the universe and huddle in implies a faith that humanity will be able to sort out its own troubles.

We are a strange breed, and the accident of our existence still awes us to the core. Our ingenuity throughout the ages still surprises us, and though there may be no hope for us in the long run, if we were to accept our isolation in the universe, and our lonely post among the stars, it does belie a certain willingness to see things as they are, and grab the bull of life by the horns.

***

After the introductory sequence of cosmic traverse, we are graced with what is arguably the most profound scene to date in a Muppet movie. It compares favorably to other iconic clips from the canonized classics of the medium. Among children's films, it is doubtless near the apex. Packed to bursting with symbolic riches, this densely layered sequence is a smorgasbord of analytical goodies. Probably volumes could be written on these first few minutes alone.

Yet it is not the goal here to compose these volumes. Rather, the aim is to point the way for future scholars, bright and ambitious. This essay is only a map of the places to go digging. Lade yourself with spades and trowels, ye scholars of the future, for a treasure hunt is nigh!

Having just been slung through the universe at warp speed, still moving at a clip, the camera begins to brake just as the Earth comes into view. Our planet, though recognizable, has been given the aspect of a human face. There is something troubling about its expression, for it seems to exhibit the half-palsied droop of a stroke victim. Its blubbering humanoid expression inspires instinctual revulsion, and we can't help but associate the planet as a whole with the infirmity of its most sickly inhabitant, the human being. Diseased and disabled, our own sickness seems to have tainted the entire globe.

Looking closer, we notice the familiar landmasses are oddly arranged, smashed together into a single continent. Evoking thoughts of Pangaea, the hypothetical conjunction of all seven continents into one unified body, we are to understand that mankind is united across borders and cultures in the plight of modernity.

Though the decay of bedrock institutions is thought to be a primarily Western phenomenon, this is hardly the case. Modernization occurs in every nation, and lands as far-flung as India and Brazil now enter the dark world we Westerns have called home since the birth of the modern era. Europeans, being the first of the world's nations to industrialize, were arguably the first to feel the ground give way beneath their feet; but the fracturing of traditional perspectives is underway everywhere, no exemptions.

Zeroing in on what would be the right eye of this half-paralyzed face, we are shocked to find it a swirling chaos. A window into the soul, indeed. Plunging deeper, we find ourselves at the calm center of a titanic hurricane. Lightning bolts blaze brightly across the churning clouds. The wind whips, and birds struggle to maintain themselves aloft. There is a sense that something terrible is about to be born—a beast both monstrous and awe-inspiring. Something mythic is on the verge of occurring, the seed for an epic tale that will resonate through humanity's soul for eons to come, told about in books and whispered about around hearths and campfires.

This is only the first of many birth-related symbols we'll encounter in this scene. These first few minutes are practically an ocean of hearty amniotic soup, and we're invited to dip our ladles in deep. We need only apply our scholarly forceps to the head that is crowning, and act as midwife to the notions struggling to be born. Who here wants to practice obstetrics of a more academic sort?

Raise your hand, ye scholars, ye doulas, ye deliverers of fresh babes!

If it seems a stretch that violent bursts of lightning would reference the grueling pangs of birth, we need only take a moment and consider the role lightning played in the formation of organic life. In the beginning, there was naught but molecules and minerals, raw material for cellular life. By the electrified strokes of lightning, surging deep into this moist primordial stew, amino acids were forged. This set the stage for proteins and later, single-celled organisms, which through the millennia would evolve into the wealth of life forms we behold in our present day.

Though scientists still debate the particulars of this theory, there is little doubt that some variation of the process occurred. Regardless of accuracy, the theory comprises a healthy portion of our own secular and scientific "creation myth." This is our Genesis moment, when terrestrial Life itself drew its first gasping breath.

Curiously, after one particularly brutal clap of lightning, what appears to be a lion cub slowly forms out of the churning morass. Yes, a lion cub. Some may argue that I'm unjustifiably projecting shapes onto the clouds, like a sky-gazing child whimsically passing a sunny afternoon. Absolutely not. I would happily, at any time, point out the very clear neonatal outline of the blonde beast, and bring the battle to any naysayers. The reader must understand that the last thing I was looking for in this sky was a lion cub. I was truly dumbfounded by what I saw coming into definition on the screen, and confounded as to the possible implications.

Concerned that I was merely interjecting my own associations onto a blank and amorphous slate, I retired to a sink basin and splashed my face with cold, invigorating water from the tap. Even the sharpest of analysts will from time to time require a freshening respite before tackling his project anew. Returning to my monitor I rubbed my eyes and looked again. At this point the matter was confirmed. This was a lion cub, and the matter was no longer in doubt. And however strange this creature in the clouds might seem to others, I immediately recognized the significance.

In what is probably Nietzsche's most famous book, the biblically structured *Thus Spake Zarathustra*, there are said to be three metamorphoses on the journey towards a flourishing spiritual life. These stages point the way towards Nietzsche's hypothetical Overman, who will transcend humanity altogether, sloughing off its congenital weaknesses like an ape molting into a god.

This so-called Overman will move beyond history and its endowment, creating his own values and dictating his own morality. An aristocratic being, he will discover his own good and evil, measured against only what is beneficial to his own life and completeness. He will have no use for morbid notions like sin or guilt, and having freed himself of resentment towards life, will affirm the goodness of existence without reserve. It is the death of God that creates the vacuum necessary for the Overman's birth.

According to Nietzsche, before we can take our first step toward becoming this wondrous Overman, we must transform into camels. A beast of burden, the camel consciously takes upon itself the heaping weight of humanity's collective experience. Aye, his very spine comes close to snapping in twain. He accepts the baggage of our gloomy past upon his humped back, our misfires and false starts, and all the energy misspent plodding our way down philosophical dead ends. Quiet and unassuming, the camel immerses himself in the accumulated learning of history's renowned sages and scientists. Beyond this, he bears up the tragic onus of the human condition itself, unwilling to shrug off the terrible aspect of our kind's existential reality. Thus laded, the camel roams the desert, bypassing the false oases that promise momentary, but illusory, refuge from the arid wasteland through which he wanders.

While adrift in this desert, and when the time is ripe, the camel is compelled to undergo another transformation. His burden is absorbed into his very being, and he morphs into a lion.

This blonde beast affirms the deepest truth of the modern era, the Death of God, and accepts the profound responsibility of freedom implied by this event. By doing so he opens the door to the limitless possibilities of his own spiritual freedom. This lion has but one task, to slay the dragon called Thou Shalt, who seeks to impose an outside morality upon the golden-haired lion. When we accept that a true morality cannot come from outsides ourselves or be dictated to us; when we wholly affirm that a proper morality must be a positive, blossoming, organic outgrowth from ourselves, not an external set of codes and laws, we will have murdered the scaly beast. The dragon lays bleeding under our clawed paws.

Defeating the dragon Thou Shalt is not enough, however. It is only one more step on the quest toward the Overman. The lion is still a reactive creature; a destroyer, not a creator. And so the blonde beast must transform into a child. Like a child at play, he must creatively experiment with new moralities and spiritual approaches. He does so with innocence and sporting zest.

The child still has purity and doesn't take life too seriously. He is experimental and curious. He wants to test boundaries and explore novelties. Improvisational and flexible, at least ideally, the child has not had his instincts corrupted by the religious and social institutions around him. He is free to try new things, to dance in the daisies and feel joy at the endless varieties and potentials of life, and to avoid at all costs the caged-in lives of the jaded elders who surround him.

***

By the time we are introduced to Gonzo, he is very clearly mired down in the so-called Stage of the Camel. He has pulled the cataracts from his eyes and beholds the world with no filtering veil. It is an awful kind of clarity, and in no way conducive to health of mind. His insights have somehow pushed him away from the world, and imprisoned him in a hellish sequestration. Not only have his friends and fellows became alien to him, but the entire world he inhabits now comes across as a terrible nightmare.

No doubt most higher spirits have experienced this peculiar sense of amputation from the very reality they inhabit. Knowing themselves to be physically woven into the world's mesh, yet in some kind of free-float away from it, like a helium balloon wafting further and further from the Earth's firm surface. This feeling can be horrific, and exposes whoever is burdened by it to a nihilistic gloom. One doesn't know where to turn, what to do, or how to seek a resolution. Many turn to suicide, religion, or novelty cults. Alcohol, drugs, and entertaining diversions often serve as indispensable distractions from the truth we find so indigestible.

Those of a skeptical bent, however, often find themselves suspended in limbo. They go through the motions of life hoping someone or something will rescue them from their own dark self. If we are not destroyed by our responses to the gloom of reality, we must soberly face the cold facts and make decisions, the ones we have been putting off. This is the goal of the camel: to willfully and purposefully accept the burden he is already been loaded down with. And then, to increase that burden. To know lucidly and soberly what that burden is, and then to carry it with him until he is ready to take decisive action to relieve it, to shrug it off.

All this of course in a way that affirms the value of life. No suicide or chemical oblivion allowed.

***

The camera begins to pan lower, dropping from the violent skies to the oddly desiccated landscape below. We are treated here to a subtle but fascinatingly poignant image. No doubt very few viewers have made note of this image, whether they be analysts or passive fans of the film. But as always, it is our duty as adventurers in film theory to notice what others do not, and to bravely venture where others have either no interest or no inclination.

Just as it comes to a stop at eye-level, the camera focuses for some brief but suggestively lingering length of time on a charred branch. We must look through and beyond this charred branch to see the world beyond. Why? What exactly is occurring here?

Now, it seems to me that nobody could argue against me in this. To my eyes, the charred branch looks far less like a scorched tree limb than it does the charred forearm of a human being, burnt to a crisp. This is eerie. Seeing charred human bodies—or indeed the charred remains of any creature—is always an unpleasant sight. Why is this? What about charred bodies is particularly despicable to us? I don't know. Perhaps it comes from some primal fear of fire, passed down to us through genetic inheritance.

Within the context, we are reminded of Michelangelo's famous painting on the ceiling of the Sistine Chapel, *The Creation of Adam*. In this iconic work, God is depicted reaching out to Adam, and Adam reaching back. The tips of their fingers come near to touching, but there still remains a gap. It is said that between this gap the spark of life is transmitted to the newly created human being. Somehow this spark seems to have ignited the divine creator, and a conflagration was started in Heaven.

Interestingly, what appears to be a small, cloaked figure walks along the scorched length of the outstretched finger. The elongated beak gives the figure away as Gonzo, dolled up in monk's robes. This image declares to us that Gonzo seeks nothing but communion with the traditional God of Christianity, or at least some traditional conception of God. But God is clearly dead, burnt to a shriveled and twisted wreck, and Gonzo seeks communion with a being that has long shed His mortal coil. It might also be read that Gonzo's climb toward God is with the intention of taking his place, and becoming a God unto himself, or at least taking over the role God would once have had in his life. The tiny Gonzo may or may not be aware that the God he seeks is dead, but he must certainly have his suspicions.

It's certainly no coincidence that the Death of God be associated with Noah's Ark. Though the story, told as it is from Noah's perspective, seems to advocate for a certain trust in God, it seems clear that were the story told from the perspective of those left behind it would have very different insinuations. We're told that the inhabitants of the Earth had become very wicked, and had turned from God. In some ways this describes the world of today.

Faith in God has diminished, and though life is generally good, wickedness abounds across the seven continents. Though God opts to choose a very tiny group for salvation, the rest of us are condemned to drown in the floodwaters.

No amount of pleading or prayer can save them, and God is deaf to their cries. Crisis is everywhere today, and in the background we know that this Earth has a destiny with doom. Like our own lives, its death has been written into its very existence.

Oddly perhaps, while this apocalyptic storm is still only brewing on the horizon, this world is already post-apocalyptic in the details. The blasted landscape is dead earth and clear-cut trees. The soil is ash, and it seems as if the world has already been destroyed.

What can we take from this? The world as we know it is clearly not a barren place. Not physically, anyway. Yes, of course we can all point to factories, smog, the blight of strip-mined and forested hillsides. But generally speaking, what do we see all around us? The beauty of the natural world. Being that I live in a small arts town in the Rocky Mountains, it would be easy to accuse me of ignorance. Yes, I live in a beautiful place. But I have lived in cities, from Seattle to New York, and the beauty of the natural world was everywhere. The mountains and the streams and the parks we build our cities around. In general, it is very easy to find the solicitous beauty of the natural world.

So why, if the Earth is still beautiful in a general way, should *Muppets From Space* depict it as a wasteland? Well, men may physically exist in the natural world, but the world we really live in is our own heads. The "real world" is a mental construct created symbiotically between our minds and physical reality. Our minds accept sensory data and build a picture of the world, a complex reflection of our mental biases. The mind shapes the world. It is not so much our physical world that is a wasteland, but our mental and social world. It is literally in ruins. It is a desert. Our human soul is a desiccated and polluted place. How people find a home here is unbelievable, for there is no purpose.

For most people, children become the purpose of their lives. This is not a bad thing, because without children most people would not be able to find a purpose. Careers and that sort of thing are sold to us as being alternative sources of purpose. This might be true for a very few, but how many of us find true purpose in our careers? What matters most in our lives is the people that populate it. Friends and relatives and chance acquaintances.

***

Within the mythical narrative of Noah's Ark, the storming clouds are the very literal expression of God's wrath, soon to be visited upon the hapless inhabitants of Earth. However, in this film the clouds represent the Age of Disbelief that is encroaching. God's aloofness, or His absence, is seen as the very deluge that will lay the world asunder. God's non-existence is more terrifying than his anger. They say that the opposite of love is not hate, but indifference. A scolded child still knows he is loved, that some being he trusts cares enough to correct his behavior. But if a child acts up and finds himself pushing against boundaries that do not exist, he becomes fretful. An angry voice is still a voice, and for that reason is a comfort. Howling silence distresses more than a bellowing rage.

From every corner of this world, panicked animals are running toward the refuge of Noah's Ark.

That these animals are running through a ravaged no-man's land provides an interesting clue to unlocking the film's themes. The destruction of the Earth, according to the flood narrative, has not even occurred. But here in the film, the Earth is already scourged, a place of carnage and destruction, long-ruined by negligent hands. What we gather is that Earth was never really a wholesome home for the heart of man to begin with.

Consciousness was never meant to grow here, or at least should not have been part of the plan. For inhabitants of Earth, awareness is the weightiest of curses. True awareness, true knowledge of ourselves, is a recipe for madness. Furthermore, we see that nature itself is as much our enemy. Asteroids, pathogens, super-storms, and the like acutely demonstrate that we are but mites, our existence accidental and perilous in the extreme. The sweeping scythe of Death will soon go thrashing cross the Earth, mowing down its unsuspecting populace without prejudice or mercy.

Gonzo too struggles across the blasted landscape, and may be just a split-second too tardy to secure a cabin on Noah's legendary barge.

Though at this time God was only chastising the Earth, and cleansing it of what he considered its filth, the very idea that God would destroy the Earth inspires some difficult questions. It is one of those things that make us question not only the nature, but the very existence of God. Why would

He make this universe, and this world, full of creatures created in His very own image, if all of it is destined to wind up destroyed?

The sun dies, there are galaxies headed toward our own in an inevitable collision course. Why would God build this entire world, so full of storm and stress, sound and fury, if in the end it really signified nothing? It behooves believers to argue that this window of existence provides plenty of time for God's plan for us to unfold. Perhaps. But why the destruction of so many species, and why such buildup? It is estimated that likely ninety-nine percent or more of all the species that have inhabited Earth have sloughed off the mortal coil, and exist no more.

***

We are here treated to another indication that we are watching what is simultaneously and exploration of death and birth. As Gonzo stumbles over the ruined landscape towards the welcoming glow of a lantern hung beside the hatch of the Ark, he screams, "I'm coming! I'm coming!" This is of course the ecstatic and orgasmic scream of someone in the throes of ejaculation.

In the way that dreams and real life intersect, it would appear that Gonzo is ejaculating in his sleep, his sticky emissions blasting into the flannel of his pajamas. This dark, nightmarish dream is actually erotic in some profound way. Shooting our seed wastefully, away from the soil of the womb, is generally considered masturbatory and in no way an act of fertilization. But Gonzo's ejaculation is not of this kind.

He will in fact be giving birth to a newer version of himself, and it is the Death of God that has allowed him this opportunity for rearing the child that exists within his own soul.

Finally arriving at the Ark, Gonzo finds himself in line behind a group of sheep hoofing their way up the ramp. It's hardly surprising Gonzo will not be allowed on board. How could he find a place of comfort amongst herding beasts? It is the herd mentality that he must escape from in order to transcend his condition. Aside from the obvious association with sheep as animals who are easily led and prone to a pernicious groupthink, Nietzsche used these congenial ruminants in an illustration of herd morality. The sheep calls the eagle evil because the eagle is prone to swoop down and carry off their lambs. But an eagle is only acting according to its nature. By denying God and traditional religion, Gonzo has already accepted his own "wickedness."

Still, Gonzo at this point feels nothing but isolation, and seeks the companionship and emotional safety of the herd. Approaching Noah, Gonzo begs entrance of the full-bearded Hebrew. Noah is aghast, interrogating Gonzo both about his opposite female number, and attacking his claims to the title of animal. Tasked by God to save only known species, he demands Gonzo answer the unanswerable question: "What are you?"

To pitiless Noah, Gonzo is unfit for redemption. He lacks in two categories: he is the only one of his kind, and knows not what he is. It is here we know that Gonzo is the ultimate metaphor for humankind. A sentient being without a true context for his existence, yet having to weave a narrative about himself from out of his own creative mind.

Though I had always assumed Gonzo to be some kind of flightless bird, within the Hensonian Muppet mythos he is apparently not a species of terrestrial origin. Prior to this film, there had been no accounting whatsoever of his origins. He was a cipher and non-entity. A weirdo.

Mythology is an explanatory narrative humans use to explain our origins, and Gonzo is poverty-stricken in this regard. He has stepped outside the stream of all mythologies, and has no stories to explain his own existence in the world. A question mark is branded upon his forehead. What is he, other than a weirdo? For a long time nobody even bothered to ask. It was his inexplicability that finally became the surface upon which the scriptwriters projected their own religious unease. In this sense, Gonzo was always destined to be the vessel for which his creators would voice their own existential anxieties.

With blunt and belligerent force, Noah asks, "What are you? What species?" Why this aggression? So much is said by this attitude, which is perfectly reflective of a pernicious concept in all religions, the idea of The Elect. Among the most potent psychological tools of groupthink is the nurturance of elitism among the flock. To those of us who are mostly looking for a shepherd or leader, the idea that we are special, that we are adherents to an exclusive ideology, that we alone are the sacred and saved, is the glue that binds us to a creed that might otherwise come under intense scrutiny. This is among the strangest attributes of religion, and something those who find arbitrary exclusion distasteful. We are the saved, and you are the damned! And all according to criteria settled upon by the saved. Why most people need, and indeed feed off of, this prejudice against others is a mystery about our kind's psychological makeup.

Gonzo admits to Noah that he doesn't know what he is. Though he finds the criteria unjust, he acknowledges that it is the set criteria. And so disqualifying Gonzo for deliverance from the deluge, Noah rudely shuts the hatch. Gonzo's face sinks, but is alit by a bright glimmer of hope when Noah reemerges. Hope blazes in his eyes, but is extinguished for good when he is callously handed an umbrella.

The flippancy with which he is regarded is actually typical. The most devoted religionist easily dehumanizes those outside their clique or tribe. People with alien beliefs are regarded as mere chaff, and those who believe nothing are seen as apostates, not lonesome questioners who have exposed their very souls to the vulnerability of independent thought. Because group establishment is only partly familial in our society, we compensate by submitting to an ideological kinship. Common belief takes the place of common relations, and we cement our tribal affiliations with strange theologies.

Humanity is itself the ultimate cipher and unexplained phenomena. Gonzo's abandonment is the worst kind of nightmare because he has been left utterly alone to perish obscurely on chastised Earth. But aren't we ourselves burdened by this very fate? Humanity is alone in the universe, dumbfounded by the very reality of our existence, and the uncertainties that haunt us.

Gonzo turns to survey the deathly, barren landscape before him. It is not suggested he is left behind to endure punishment with the rest of Earth's wicked souls. Even the wicked are company of a kind, and would be welcomed by a person suffering loneliness. Indeed, it seems as if the entirety of Earth's residency has been included on Noah's Ark, and it is isolation, even in doom, that Gonzo is tormented by. By the same token, we are encouraged to associate Gonzo with the wicked, at least as outlined in the myth of Noah's Ark. It is indeed an evil impulse, which will bring us to deny God.

Nietzsche famously advocated for the utility of what was popularly regarded as evil. Wickedness has its uses, and the vices such as cruelty, hatred, and anger can be sublimated to achieve noble ends. In coming to know ourselves, and shed the religious ideology that has for eons kept us from truly knowing ourselves, many of us will feel that we are acting out of some evil impulse.

To deny God is rarely a comfortable experience, and atheism will likely engender a great deal of anxiety and guilt. We must work our way through this, and recognize it as a danger. Guilt about disbelief has, after all, been the favorite tool of religion all along for ensuring conformity amongst the ranks, and stamping out the fire of independent thought.

Above all else, this powerful segment of the film suggests the inability of traditional Judeo-Christian mythology—or indeed any religion formulated in the past eons of humanity's ignorant youth—to guide us through the pitfalls of the modern malaise.

How can a religious creed formed in the mostly illiterate boroughs of the Middle East possibly address the concerns of a sophisticated civilization such as ours? Religious thought is most fascinating, perhaps, for its ubiquity in the modern world. A relic from our benighted past, it nevertheless lives with us today as an anachronism. For all the revolutionary changes civilization has undergone, humanity remains unchanged in its fundamental makeup. The chimp has risen to dizzying heights, but remains for all that a confused ape.

So we cling to our past, even as time drags us inexorably away from the spiritual comforts of our ancestors. As we are hurled into the future, though, the old explanations will become less and less satisfying, and less believable. We are almost there now, and the hunger for new paradigms is palpable everywhere. As we've discussed, the scientific alternative offers little in the way of hope or optimism. And so we attempt to formulate a story about ourselves that incorporates the knowledge of science, but allays its dismal conclusions.

Gonzo turns to the sky as the rains begin to fall. He delivers the bellow that is all mankind's primal scream, aimed upward at the heavens, addressed to God Himself: "I don't want to be alone!"

His lament is hurled against the uncaring world, which remains deaf to his cries. The words echo and reverberate not only into the next scene of the film, but through our very souls. Absence a divine shepherd, humanity must accept the burden of cosmic solitude. We are utterly alone, working without a net, uncertain as to how we should proceed. No meaning can be read in Nature, and God has no messages for us. All is randomness and cruelty.

The entire historical framework justifying our morality and explaining our destiny has been pulled from beneath our feet. We hover over an abyss, afraid to look down lest we drop into the bottomless nothing. Gonzo's aloneness and isolation is social as well as metaphysical, his primal scream a frightening verbalization of cosmic terror.

God is dead, the Earth will die, and we will not have known our origins, nor even the meaning of our existence, provided there is one (which hardly seems likely). We will not have answered those three eternal questions, most famously expressed by the French painter, Gaugin: "Where do we come from? What are we? Where are we going?"

***

Unsettled in his bed, Gonzo shudders and shakes. He appears to be having an orgasm—as he screamed in his dream, he is indeed "coming."

The hearty ejaculate that will be the seed from which his transcendent self must grow spews forth into his pajamas. Quite tellingly, the pajamas Gonzo wears are patterned with birds. Birds remind us of one of the Earth's great extinctions, the death of the dinosaurs.

Throughout this first section of the film, there is obsession with extinction, with the end of a genetic line and the finality of death. The ability to reproduce is fundamentally intertwined with our self worth as beings. It is a fundamental building block of purpose. Those who consciously forego children frequently do so with an aim toward other kinds of productive behavior, such as in their career or the life of the mind; in science and philosophy. But the death of the dinosaurs conjures up in us notions of our own precarious place within existence.

Chance occurrences can, and indeed one day will, bring this all to a dead end. That is the future. That is ordained. How we cope with the truth of our own extinction—as individual persons and as a species—illustrates what we are able to make of this world and this life in the face of certain annihilation.

As Gonzo bolts upright from his soul-shaking slumbers, he screams once more to the world at large, "I don't want to be alone!" In so doing, he knocks his roommate, the bellicose and jovial rat Rizzo, out of his overhead hammock and out the window.

Defenestration—being tossed from a window—has a historical association with religious and political rebellion. The term comes from the Defenestration of Prague, two separate incidents in which noblemen were tossed from castle windows. The political rebellion was also religious, and had to do with the outlawing of Protestantism by what was considered to be a Catholic usurper. This is conceptually attached to a rebellion from imposed religious forms, and also connects to a distinction between Gonzo's psychology and Rizzo's, as will be discussed below.

Gonzo gets up and helps Rizzo back inside. Being told that Gonzo has once more experienced his recurring dream, Rizzo flippantly asks Gonzo if it was "the one with the goat, dwarf, and a jar of peanut butter." This crude sexual innuendo—for what else can it be?—exposes Gonzo's dream-life to a higher level of analysis.

On the surface it comes across merely as an adult joke calculated to fly over the heads of children and hit parents smack dab in their funny bones. But its function is manifold and highly sophisticated, comparing favorably to the subtlest maneuvers in the cinematic arts. Besides making us laugh, and heartily, Rizzo's joke confirms that there are aspects of the film addressing the mental life of an adult. This is a call for grown men and women to pay attention.

More importantly, Rizzo's comment fixes Gonzo's dream-life firmly to his libido. Gonzo, as a male of whatever species he happens to be, must have deeply repressed sexual urges, given that he is without a female opposite for sexual gratification. The intensity of Gonzo's need, twisted by the inability to give expression to it, has left his sexuality twisted in a Gordian knot.

Our banana-beaked hero cannot breed. This is literally true, but also figuratively. In his current psychological state, Gonzo cannot produce anything. He is impotent and infertile, unable to create any life-affirming or procreative spiritual ejaculations. His nocturnal emission was an ejaculation, yes, but for it to be more than a masturbatory squirt into his pajamas, there must be some sense of what can be birthed.

The libido is the fountainhead of sexual energy. Aside from pushing us relentlessly towards sexual gratification, it infuses our personalities from top to bottom. For Freud, this sexual energy was mostly repressed, as he hypothesized that living communally with other humans requires suppression of our strongest urges. Being Freud, he considered sexuality the absolutely dominant drive. Our inability to express it fully leads to that energy having to be sublimated and turned inward, back at us—which fosters neurosis.

Thus repressed, human beings sublimate these energies, and when channeling them healthily, they are put towards such productive social ends as civilization-building and worldly achievement.

In that sense, repression has led to the realization of humanity's greatest ambitions; but also sewed the seed for mental illness and the discontents of civilization. Jokes, for Freud, were socially acceptable expressions of taboo yearnings. They are one way in which we are allowed to safely say what's really on our mind. Dreams, of course, gave honest expression to the repressed urges and notions roiling about in the subconscious realm of our psyches.

Carl Jung, Freud's pupil and eventual rival, gave a more comprehensive definition of the libido; one less tied to the sexual instinct. Jung claimed the libido is the upwelling psychic energy of the very life processes of sentient existence, which appear to us subjectively as striving and desire. The processes of life are manifold and complicated, but aim at social and psychological wholeness, and balance between the various and frequently conflicting components of our psyche.

The goal for him was to balance the various forces of the psyche into a unified harmony, not simply to give expression to our sexual urges.

Thus Gonzo's striving to identify with the world around him, and his desire for belonging, are associated in opposition to the character Rizzo. Gonzo's yearnings are for connection with the very deepest and most primal processes of life. But by playing up Rizzo as the Freudian character who can think of nothing but sensuality and sex, it is implied that Gonzo is the vessel of Jungian concepts, wherein the libido is granted to have a higher and more spiritual aim than bestial sexual release.

Gonzo's defenestration of Rizzo was accidental, but completely appropriate in that he is rebelling against Rizzo's approach to, and conceptualization of, life.

Some foolhardy analysts may argue that Rizzo was only making an offhand remark, and that Gonzo has not in fact dreamed of goats, dwarves, or jars of peanut butter in any context, sexual or otherwise. But let us presume that Gonzo has been having this dream, as well as the other one regarding being left behind by Noah.

If Gonzo has also been dreaming of a goat, a dwarf, and a jar of peanut butter, then the symbolism can only be sexual, and if it is sexual, it arises from the deepest sectors of Gonzo's unconscious mind, presuming his psyche is structured in a similar fashion to that of a human being (a probability of which we should entertain little doubt, as Gonzo is a metaphorical stand-in for what is deeply human).

The goat is the symbol of rutting Pan, whose primary concern was to play erotically upon his flute and frolic with various nymphs in the high grasses of mountain valleys, engaging in delights too carnal for mainstream society. The dwarf symbolizes our repressed and stunted libido, whose grotesque and ribald instincts must be squashed down if mental, spiritual, and social health are to be attained. Thirdly the peanut butter, which in and of itself has no symbolic value, but can only combine meaningfully with the goat and dwarf if it is to be used by that odd pair as an instrument for perverse sexual experiences which should not even be imagined in a wholesome universe.

That established, what is the connection, if any, between Gonzo's dream of cosmic isolation and his intensely abnormal sexual longings? Without going into great theoretical detail—for such would justify an entire volume in its own right—I will here grant the reader a brief exposition of my own theory.

Here we go far beyond the comparatively objective realm of film analysis and enter the world of biased philosophical paradigm. That there are other equally compelling explanations for the connection between Gonzo's two dreams I readily admit, though I find that mine benefits greatly from a certain acuity and intellectual clarity, and is surely the product of a highly lucid mind functioning at optimum levels.

I would begin by positing that the Death of God as a historical event represents the highest kind of spiritual crisis for collective humanity. Belief in God is ingrained in our social and psychological existence as human beings, and atheism has been statistically non-existent throughout our history. It has only begun to emerge as a social movement in the last decade or two, and a fragmented one at that. The prominence of public debates between public intellectuals who are atheists, and their frequent appearance on popular news programs, suggests a guilty fascination and dalliance. That religious reactionaries are so vehement in addressing the growing irreligiousness of society shows that they consider it a persuasive threat.

For all the confidence in the rightness of their positions, atheists fight for a Pyrrhic victory—one in which the losses are so extreme that true victory cannot be claimed. To deny the existence of God is in fact a rebellion against our own hardwiring, our very own selves; and therein lay the crisis. It may seem to the atheist that his rejection of religious beliefs is primarily social. Religious concepts have been imposed on him from an outside source, which he then rejects on account of his reason.

However, even just to entertain a godless universe is the first volley in a war against not only our own hearts and minds, but against the heart and mind of our species. It is to wage war against our own evolutionary history. One has immediately put oneself in opposition to billions of years of biological development, and tens of thousands of years of civilized advancement. It's enough to make even the bravest of us fearful, and the largest of us to feel small and insignificant.

To declare one's doubt in the divine is to sow the seeds of a bad conscience. I am quite certain that even if atheism were not explicitly sinful in the eyes of the world's religions, we would still feel guilt at declaring ourselves free of such superstition. Indeed, if religious belief is considered even slightly adaptive in an evolutionary sense; and if we accept that religious concepts grow out of the baser instincts of a simian; we can easily accept that there is a suicidal note to atheism.

Today, atheists are increasingly vocal and confident in their stance, and frequently provide forums to advance and argue their views. However, they are still mostly regarded as dangerous curiosities by the mass media, as well as by the viewer who is fascinated by their heresy. They are the mouthpieces for a dangerous apostasy, and our interest in them is the same as our interest in serial killers and mass murderers. It is a macabre fascination, and even if we too are atheists, we are made anxious by the fact that atheists and atheism exist; and even that we exist as atheists.

The great mass of humanity is still religious, and it may be that atheism and agnosticism are primarily the luxuries of affluent societies. When our fortunes don't seem so capricious or fleeting, and we maintain a certain amount of control over our physical environment, we allow ourselves a little hubris. It is when we are standing on thin ice that we become most susceptible to belief. As the old chestnut goes, there are no atheists in a foxhole.

Oddly, this maxim has always seemed much more to discount belief in God than advocate for it, as religious people tend to presume. What it suggests is that we believe in God because we are afraid. When we are in real danger, when we seem least in control, we petition a God to oversee our wellbeing, and to guide us through whatever dangers are causing us the greatest amount of angst.

The real devil for us has always been uncertainty, and we've wrestled with this evil spirit since our inception. Not just as modern humans, but as proto-humans, and even as simpler forms than that. Probably anxiety is the real bedrock of consciousness; anxiety concerning food, shelter, predators, and so on. Have any of us living beings ever been allowed to simply relax and be happy? How many millions of generations have sought a psychological comfort that never arrives? Even today, in our wealthiest societies, there is no relaxing. Wars, poverty, natural disasters; economic and environmental collapse: all these worries are the white noise we live in—it is a constant buzzing sound.

It is the tendency of non-believers to view the rise of religion as a mistake. What began as an incorrect assumption about reality was institutionalized, and was then perpetuated by those who benefited from its belief. But belief must have lent us some evolutionary advantage in our "tooth-and-claw" past.

God, if not strictly construed as either an entity or personality, is a projection born of some peculiar human need. Loosely conceived, God is equivalent to a sense of transcendent purpose. A society has achieved the ultimate cohesion when its members all worship the same God or pantheon of gods, and every individual in that society entertains a homogenous conception of that God or those gods.

In that case, not necessarily God, but a belief and understanding of God held communally, is a social adhesive binding one person to another, and each to all. It also serves to justify the structure and even the very existence of a given society. A healthy civilization requires a "God" of some kind, a salient reason for individual members of a community to promote in their personal actions the general wellbeing of that selfsame community.

Rewarding desired behaviors with money and prestige is simply not enough to sustain the greatest spirits in a population, and a society ill-serves itself if their greatest type is crippled by nihilism and pessimistic melancholy. In brief, the reason the concept God exists is to justify the existence of a community to itself. This function becomes more complex in a secular democratic culture like our own, wherein people are allowed their own definition of God, but the proposition still holds true.

When the general trend of decay begins in a civilization, its God also dies. It is no coincidence that as our society becomes more fragmented, atheism has become more popular. What is cause and what is effect is debatable, whether the loss of God causes decay or decay causes the loss of God, but the two are opposite sides of the same coin. But happily for our purposes, we do not require a solution to that problem. If a God dying leads to decay, so be it. If decay leads to the Death of God, let it be taken for granted and nothing more.

This point established beyond dispute, we must now turn to the most natural, or at least most common, human responses to the Death of God.

There may be strenuous denials, as are numerous beyond enumerating in our day, from Biblical Literalism to New Age Chicanery. These efforts to affirm dubious religious modes and to reaffirm ideologies that are incompatible with the modern paradigm, is in fact the most obvious indicators that we are in crisis. A spiritually healthy populace is not reactionary in this way, and doesn't try to force an ideology onto a pedestal from which it has supposedly fallen. That there are many among us who seek to reassert spirituality suggests a growing need for belief of some kind, even if that belief is far out of step with where we are at as a civilization.

Perhaps a more common reaction to the spiritual void, is when a people reverts to desperate attempts at ecstasy; the loss of one's self in some activity. For some it is drugs, for others work or entertainments, alcohol, athletic activity, and medication through Zoloft and similar psychotropic drugs. But the most general response—probably because it also serves the commercial interests of our economic system—is a morbid obsession with sexuality, the original ecstatic experience.

Primarily, the obsession is with sexuality divorced from procreation, a development practically unimaginable in other epochs of human history.

That our age craves ever greater sexual libertinage is a sign indeed that any notion of transcendent purpose is completely lacking, and that where its existence is not utterly lacking—in the Churches, for instance—it nevertheless lacks utter credibility. Freud maintained that repression of the sexual instinct is necessary to the proper functioning of a civilization, but that it creates a general discontent.

Perhaps Gonzo's "return of the repressed," as evidenced by the perverted sexual nature of his dream-life, signals a coming eruption of unconscious tensions into the conscious mind, as Gonzo labors under the burden of the isolated, alienated existence that the modern world imposes.

That Gonzo has a deep-seated appetite for some of the most decadent sensual indulgences—bestiality, group sex, polyamorous dwarf-play—is merely to indicate his complete isolation from traditional concepts of God, or at least his dangerous proximity to the most extreme states of nihilism.

The procreative act is no longer for procreation, but for recreation and experimentation. In the Western world, where the traditional concepts of God are most decayed, our birth rates are declining. There is almost no country in the Western hemisphere in which the birth rates are high enough to sustain the native population.

Religious pundits point out, quite rightly, that the decline in birth rates is a product of nihilism, and a general lack of faith in the future. Libertinage is indeed a sign that a civilization is near the end of its rope. As Nietzsche pointed out, libertinage is not a cause of decadence, but one of its most telling symptoms. Sensual indulgence and gluttony are signs that the end is nigh, the people are exhausted, and require constant stimulation just to keep going another day.

***

While Gonzo tries once more to communicate the intensity of feeling his dream has inspired, bored Rizzo falls asleep. If Gonzo needed confirmation of how estranged from his peers his yearnings make him, Rizzo's gentle snores are surely that confirmation.

Gonzo's concerns are not the concerns of the many. They are a burden uniquely reserved for those of heightened spiritual sensitivity. Rizzo is a mediocre spirit, a mere sensualist. So long as his base carnal needs are met, so long as his appetites find satisfaction, he is happy. He seeks no more enduring or richer sustenance from life, nor a deeper happiness. He will live and die without asking why or what it all was for; at peace with the world.

It would be an understatement to suggest that not everyone has the inclinations of a Plato or Plotinus, Spinoza or St. John of the Cross. These famous names stand apart from history precisely because of their exceptional natures, not in spite of them. Throughout the life of our species, there have always been "the masses," whose members stand as a kind of foil to spiritual seekers.

Without succumbing to elitism, it is wise to remember that most people are hardly capable of achieving a half-retarded spiritual awakening, and are content to regurgitate the thoughts of the self-proclaimed spiritual authorities found in their communities and in the mass media. They are cattle, wanting only to be driven in some particular direction by somebody who proclaims a destination. Their favorite place is the corral, where they safely blend in with the group.

Souls burdened by deep thoughts may envy the dullard's approach to life's mysteries, but will find no success in trying to imitate that shallowness. Once the big questions of purpose arise in our minds there is no ignoring them ever again—at least not without serious psychological and emotional ramifications. What is repressed by force will always return.

Those who cannot ignore questions of purpose and meaning, those ones who are sensitive to the gloominess of modern life, will often find themselves isolated. They feel uncomfortable bringing up morbid notions with friends and family. To blend in, they succumb to the social pressures demanding they remain forever congenial and in good spirits.

This is not to criticize, for the melancholy soul needs release from the weight of his thoughts, and much more so than the average person. But these respites into good company, and good times, can never bridge the two types or bring them together. The differences in mentality and orientation are, in the end, too great.

The average man's typical stance vis-a-vis a true spiritual seeker is to stand staring bug-eyed at him, jaws agape. A deep soul can still feel affection for those who don't share his inclinations, but a shallow soul is disturbed and turned off by a thinker. Thoughts they've never had, or don't understand, can make them dismissive or even hostile. A doubt about God, or the meaning of life, will provoke an angry attack, as if casting a critical eye on common prejudices was a personal insult. They brush off the philosopher as a malcontented kook, or an eccentric.

What they hardly ever do is take his speculations seriously in and of themselves, though they may take them seriously as a sign of a personality disorder. This is only natural. The chief aim of the commoner is to go about his business unburdened by discomforting thoughts.

The Gonzos of the world shall ever remain incomprehensible to the Rizzos, and the Rizzos to the Gonzos.

Though it's easy to lament this state of affairs, the budding philosopher should perhaps take heart. Things may all be as they should. To invite the merely average person into the world of spiritual speculation is to let goats run roughshod in the temple, where they are liable to trample and gnaw at the sacred parchments.

As Nietzsche was wont to point out, the philosopher of the future requires a certain amount of contempt, and a realistic evaluation of rank. Those who are beneath them need to be recognized as belonging to a lower order. What humanity needs now is the soaring eagle, not the rutting goat. The goats are many, and the eagles few. The sharp, piercing caw of these noble birds will be drowned out by the loose-lipped blabbering and bleating of the goats.

If all this smacks of tasteless elitism, remember that Nietzsche insists the higher spirit have greater contempt for himself than for the sheep he is surrounded by. He must look into his own soul and excise the weaknesses and pathetic elements within. His task is far more difficult than the average soul's is, and his burden heavier. He must respect and despise himself in equal measure. But it is by recognizing the gulf between singular persons and the great swell of the masses that allows those functioning at a higher level to find the confidence to soar.

By allowing themselves the slight condescension, the slight sense of superiority, they can allow themselves a higher purpose in life. Even if this all becomes bloated and self-important egoism—delusional to the core—those who truly do have something significant to offer will feel at last justified in starting their journey towards their destiny, toward that thing which only they can offer; the goal for which only their particular talents are suited.

***

Disappointed by Rizzo's cool indifference, Gonzo retires to the windowsill and stares upward, yearningly, into the black depths of space. The potted plant beside him is a shriveled and pathetic thing, having long ago withered away and died.

The dead plant is both a symptom of Gonzo's depression, indicating his disinterest in attending to regular chores; and, a symbolic representation of his soul and spirit, wasting away by slow degrees. The Great Sadness has swallowed him up entirely. If only he could be vomited out, like Jonah from the gullet of the whale, deposited upon the shores of inspired optimism and cheery countenance. But his malaise runs deep and to the very bone. He steeps in it.

Our man is drowning; the black tars of morbidity fill his straining lungs.

Depression is the word we use to describe this condition. The beak-nosed bastard is sad. We diagnose him with it, as if he were somehow an impaired thing. Depression is a disease, we are told. And being so, we think of it as something we can cure. With a little medicine, a bit of talk therapy, some regular exercise and a healthy diet of leafy greens, our Gonzo will once again be right as rain.

Psychiatrists often consider it magical thinking to assume the average person is able to "pull themselves up by the bootstraps," and so continuously lean on the easy availability of psychotropic drugs to artificially reorient the patient toward an optimistic perspective on life. For the masses, this approach may well be justified. Though depression seems to be a clear sign that we are mired in a lifestyle context that is incompatible with our true happiness, it may make more sense for some people to alter their perception of it then to alter their actual lives. It may not be practical for everyone to rearrange their lives in a way more suited to happiness, despite what our inspirational speakers might say.

Depression swoops upon us like a thirsty vampire, siphoning off the sweet juices of our animal vitality. We rage against the fatigue and lack of energy, Depression lurks like a ghoul in the shadows of our modern world. When we peer all too deeply into the discontents that make up the bulk of contemporary existence, we must be cautious. By asking questions, we are but begging to be embroiled in a quagmire of doubt and despair, and may seek in vain for the means of extricating ourselves.

For those whose depression stems from the spiritual void at the very center of our social world, it becomes all the more difficult to, as is said, pull ourselves up by the bootstraps. Our needs are philosophical and religious, and the means of addressing them tricky indeed. A proper anti-depressant would plant its seed in the deeper fathoms of our soul and grow upwards from there; but such a remedy cannot be devised in our pharmaceutical laboratories.

Americans are said to be different than almost every other culture on the globe by our faith in happiness. Officially written into our founding document by Thomas Jefferson, who famously altered political philosopher John Locke's "life, liberty, and the pursuit of property" to the broader and more ideal goal of pursuing that vague existential state of happiness, our belief that happiness is attainable is written into our cultural DNA.

Not only do we consider true happiness a realizable state, we feel in some way entitled to it. For us it is the crowning achievement of a life well-lived, and the real driving purpose behind our pursuit of wealth, security, and a fulfilling career. We make "good" decisions in an effort to rope this chimera. Eternally optimistic, we switch jobs, relocate to far-flung cities, and opt out of unfulfilling relationships, feeling to our very core that if we are not happy, we are failing to claim our inheritance.

The promise of happiness being infinitely alluring, we must ask ourselves whether there might be a way for us with more philosophical needs to attain it. Thankfully, our man Nietzsche provided a rather compelling thought experiment that has the potential to motivate us to action in pursuit of that goal.

In another of his famous aphorisms, *The Greatest Weight*, Nietzsche asks us to imagine ourselves alone at night, burdened by our dark thoughts about life and the universe. A demon steals through our window and tells us the dark secret of how the universe and time unfold in a cyclical nature.

The demon claims that there is no beginning and no end to time, and that our lives repeat endlessly for all infinity. Unlike Hindu or Buddhist concepts of reincarnation, where lives are repeated for the sake of attaining wisdom, Nietzsche's idea of The Eternal Recurrence of the Same suggests that the lives we lead occur exactly the same in every detail.

For many this is a horrifying thought. That we would experience an infinite series of lives with no hope for development or change forces us to reflect and analyze the choices we've made. Like some religions, it suggests eternal consequences for any mistakes and shortsightedness we might exhibit. For those who are generally unsatisfied with their lives, or have found it too full of suffering, disappointment, and unhappiness, death offers a satisfying release from the lackluster experience of living.

However, Nietzsche's inspiration was not to invoke despair in our hearts. Rather, this thought experiment was meant to inspire us to live the kind of life that would be worth living eternally. Even though he would later try to prove the theory rationally, he was the first to admit that it might not be true in any literal way. He did ask us to entertain the idea that it was true, though.

Suppose it were the way the universe worked? What if the idea seeped into our bones and took hold of our imaginations? What if we lived our lives as if it were true? In that case, we would be compelled to live the kinds of lives that we would not only accept living out infinitely, but would want nothing more than to experience forever.

What would this kind of life look like? It would be full of adventure, risk, and the highs and lows of visceral experience. It would be a life we were afraid to waste on jobs we hate, cities we despise, and situations that eroded our humanity.

***

But back to Gonzo's morning.

We are next treated to an entertaining montage depicting what is presumably a routine morning for this close-knit clan of marionettes. A rooster posted on the porch railing crows aloud to announce the breaking of a new dawn. All seems fresh and full of promise. Each Muppet in turn is shown to meet the new day with vigor and enthusiasm. Oh, if we could all greet the day this way! What magic must infuse these lives that they leap out of bed first thing in the morning with smiles broadcast on their faces, a song already singing in their heart.

How many of us awake this way?

Do not the great majority of us lounge about in our beds, begging short spurts of sleep from the snooze buttons on our alarm clocks? Though I do not know it for certain, I would gladly bet all my chips on the fact: those few of us who actually look forward to facing the day are not only rare diamonds, but a species altogether endangered.

Life is hard, and society has built us no home but a well-furnished cave. Knowing in our hearts that by foregoing the literal act of suicide no avenues of escape are possible, we meander through our own lives on auto-pilot, heavily plodding through the world like zombies. Take life by the horns we are told, and live it! But this convenient proscription falls deaf on our ears—we who seek ultimate answers.

And yet, the cock does crow. The sun rises again and showers its light on a brand new day. Can we afford to neglect the promise a new day brings? Are we hoary old sentimentalists by acknowledging that each morning can, by our own choices, lead to new kinds of bliss, new paths toward freedom, and an entirely new characterization of our lives? We can be reinvented, and we hold this power of invention in our own two hands. If we could only affirm this daily!

This is a profound and beautiful sentiment, though it would be easy for the jaded to miss its significance. Each new day brings an opportunity to sever ourselves from our past and create ourselves anew. We are our own potters, and able to mold ourselves into the shape we wish. This may come across as the kind of cliché we read on inspirational posters and other banal, eye-roll inducing fare. But still, how beautiful a truth! There is no reason today should be anything like yesterday. That each day begins with unlimited promise may be cliché, but it's a powerful truth.

Yesterday has no hold on us, and we need not be imprisoned by our past. Each morning offers the potential for radical and revolutionary changes in our lives. We can will ourselves up and out over the rim of whatever ruts our habits have carved out. It isn't easy to escape this worn groove and propel ourselves in alternate directions, but for those interested in making life an adventure, there is no greater exhilaration than the cawing of a nice, healthy cock.

***

We next find ourselves in the Muppet house, where they all apparently live together. This Muppet house is the real Ark, filled with young and old, and every race. The collection of animals suggests herding and civilization, from the cow to the sheep and pig. Even hunting and gathering is given nod to, with the stuffed moose head singing along with the rest of the Muppets.

The Muppet house is a standard two-story brick number, set smack-dab in a quiet middle-class neighborhood. This nondescript suburban dwelling stands in stark contrast to the Ark of Noah in terms of warmth and welcoming atmosphere. Like the Hebrew's famous vessel, its compartments are filled with all manner of startling creatures; but all are welcome and none excluded.

Home and hearth can themselves act as a fortress against God's wrath, so we are given to believe. We will see the theme endorsed time and again in this Muppet movie: that the bonds of friendship and our dearest human relations are the antidotes to the suffering inherent in the human condition. We can doubt this claim, and there are moments in the film to encourage this doubt, for even this thesis sometimes seems to come under skeptical scrutiny. Yet many of us will perhaps find the wholeness we seek in our comrades and fellow voyagers.

Most every Muppet from the pantheon is to be found cohabiting within these cozy walls. Characters from even minor Muppet films and television programs populate the hallways, clearly comfortable in each other's company. Those of us who are not Muppet aficionados will only have passing familiarity with many of them, showing that even the least member is a valued part of the community. Friendship is ever in bloom, and collegiality is the glue binding these rascals into a family.

Make no mistake, this hearth and home is to be understood as an Ark, a buttress against the terrible storms of life and loss. It is even promoted as more stable and sturdy than Noah's makeshift refuge. It is planted firmly in the soil, not adrift upon the waves. And when we finally get a peek at some daily goings-on, it is all to the tune of "Brick House," that timeless funk favorite penned and performed by The Commodores.

Though the lyrics of Brick House mostly contain various praises for the body measurements of some buxom sexpot, the association with impregnable stability is clear. It by no means goes beyond the bounds of reason to associate what is essentially an anthem celebrating sexuality with the comfort and utility of strong social bonds. A woman built like a "brick house" is sexually seductive at a visceral and primitive level. One need only look to ancient carvings of fertility goddesses to see that a woman so constructed is symbolically linked to our notions of rich womanhood.

Our modern sensibility has turned the more lithe and smaller pelvis of adolescent women into the sexual fetish, but it is a sexual urge divorced from procreation. The fuller-figured woman is the truest example of womanhood. What we take from this is that the family—aye, the family of man—is the hotbed of procreative potential. No man or Muppet is an island, and it is only within the social context that we are able to give birth to the highest expression of ourselves and reach our maximum potential.

And yet what is proffered as a solution to our spiritual crisis begs the question: can everyone find wholeness from their friends, family, and other human beings, or are there types who are simply unable? Though Gonzo will in the end find that he does find fulfillment in his friends and family, might this only be a necessary conclusion for a mass marketed film? Certainly none of us are lone wolves in the truest sense. As we just affirmed, it is only within the social context that any of us can truly thrive. Even those thinkers who most advocate for individualism require a society who sponsors their livelihood and publishes their works. Even the hermit who grows his own food and lives in the woods has taken those techniques from his ancestors who invented agriculture and farming. All this said, however, there will forever be among us those types who are simply unable to find in their fellows the sweet succor of true belonging. Discontented for their entire lives, other people will always be a burden to them. Does this film in the end disregard this eternally estranged type?

***

Soon after the rooster crows, we are gifted with a glimpse of four different alarm clocks ringing out the new dawn from four different nightstands. Each one is a distinct personal expression of the character awoken by it. Why were these four characters chosen, and what does each one in turn say about the approach to the freedom offered by a new day?

The first alarm clock to ring out belongs to Sam the Eagle, the Muppets embodiment of raw, all-American masculinity. The nightstand of this big-beaked patriot is adorned with miniature replicas of the Lincoln Memorial, Washington Monument, the Liberty Bell, and of course Lady Liberty herself. For Americans, these icons of political and personal freedom resonate through our very souls. They are the symbolic embodiments of our unshackled condition. Beyond political freedom, they have been used by our artists, intellectuals and sages to provoke the spiritual ambitions particular to our culture.

There is of course a kind of cynical soul who sees nothing but a brainwashed jingoism in any form of nationalism, and particularly American nationalism, as we wave the banner of freedom most loudly. But as a nationalist of sorts myself, it has long been my perspective that the American spiritual potential is the most fundamentally suited to a spirituality of the future. Though it may seem at times that we have lost contact with our spiritual roots, or wrongly presume them to be inherently Christian in character, they remain powerful tools in our spiritual arsenal. Though it may be difficult to discover them in the fog created by our mass media and overarching ideology of materialism and consumerist consumption, they are there for those who seek them out.

Writers like Melville, Therou, Emerson and others laid the groundwork for spiritual approaches that were uniquely American, conducive to our own national history and character. Moby Dick in particular, considered by most scholars to be our defining national epic, is a blueprint for the red, white, and blue spiritual seeker.

This freedom of choice of course comes with countless spiritual ramifications, and we are all often subject to the jingoistic cheers for freedom, without ever really considering the existential challenges such freedom proposes.

Second to ring out is the alarm clock of the scientist. The clock itself is some technological contraption that is hilariously complex, and built of non-digital components. It steams before a poster of the periodic table. Though we have already discussed the nihilism inherent in the scientific paradigm, we need also to understand that any spiritual approach to modernity that is worth its salt must take science and technology into consideration.

There are movements toward primitivism, but these are fundamentally regressive and reactionary approaches. A back-to-the-land mentality may be workable for some, but the primary aim is to live on the fringes of civilization, and to let it encroach on one's idyll only as necessary. A usable philosophy of the future must exist within the framework of civilization, growing organically from its stresses, strains, and upheavals.

Thirdly, we see an angry animal fist smashing a standard clock into smithereens. This is a pastiche of thematic elements that we need to disentangle to understand. First to be acknowledged is the power of the clock in our lives. Though humans have always lived according to time, from sunrise to sunset, it is the invention of the clock that sets the modern world apart from the primitive. It is the very embodiment of a rationally organized society, and is often the object of our frustrations.

There is an animalistic element inside each of us that wants to be free from the dominance of the clock. To wake naturally, to experience primitivism and freedom, and to generally rebel against the artificial breakup of the day into hours, minutes, and seconds. We achieve a certain kind of liberation by freeing ourselves from our slavish attachment to society's demands on our time. All in all, we are reminded, here and time again in the film, that we must summon the animal within ourselves to achieve freedom from the constraints on us by the herd mentality.

And then, alas, we see Kermit the Frog's nightstand and bedroom. Kermit comes across as nothing short of the archetypal fatherly patriarch of a 1950's television serial. His nightstand is neatly maintained and free of clutter. His thin green hand calmly stays his alarm and he rises up refreshed and alert. It is intended that we see him as the very picture of organic health. Green is most closely associated in our minds with bounteous and thriving life. There are plants and greenery galore in Kermit's bedroom, and his fatherly countenance compels us to consider our own fathers and the source of all being.

There are dark omens abounding though, reminding us that everything which lives must one day die. Among all this vegetative exuberance is Kermit's wallpaper, flung up on the wall behind his bed. The repeating pattern of this singular wall covering is flies, most closely associated in our minds with death and decay. His bedroom is literally covered in flies; they crawl from floor to ceiling as if over decomposing rot. Death is the end of us all, and as we look about us at this abundance of life, we are simultaneously staring at an equal amount of death. Where there is life, there is always the promise of the sorrow and mourning to come.

If this swarming of wallpaper flies were not enough for us to question the rosy façade of eternal vitality, we soon see another stark reminder of mortality. Kermit opens the door and his path is immediately crossed by a palsied, shaking elderly man rushing by with a breakfast tray held unsteadily in his hands. Cups, dishes and silverware rattle to beat the band. The tray is of a clearly institutional sort, of the kind found in cafeterias, hospitals, and nursing homes. Most interestingly, Kermit briefly looks out his door at the white-haired, wild-eyed octogenarian rumbling by. Yet he quickly looks down and ties his bathrobe, as if purposefully avoiding eye contact with the elderly man.

What exactly is he shying away from? Our own demise haunts us at every step, and what we desire more than anything is to never die. What clearer sign of our own desire to remove aging and death from our sight is there than the American nursing home? The aged and infirm wile away the twilight years of their lives in isolation. They wait to die, and we let them wait. If suicide were sanctioned in our culture, how many of these sad souls would bring themselves to a swift and merciless end.

Instead, they linger. And we pretend they do not exist, so that we are able to maintain the course after our own pursuits. The famous tale of the Buddha claims that he was a wealthy prince, insulated from the suffering of those outside his wall. He left the royal compound one day and encountered a sick man, and old man, and a dead man. This was enough for him to immediately abandon his privileged post and all its trappings, and spend the rest of his days pursuing spiritual enlightenment. Could it be that our willful sequester from the aged and dying is our effort to remain blissfully ignorant inside the walls of our own palace?

For the next five minutes, we are shown the banal morning routines of countless Muppets. Few films make so much of these routine activities, or capture them with such loving detail. These scenes perform a multitude of functions, and again, expose us to many levels of interpretation. On the one hand, we are reminded that the human person takes maintenance. We must pay attention to ourselves. Moreover, a healthy body leads to a healthy mind, which leads to healthy thoughts. Nietzsche believed the reason so many philosophers were pessimistic was a result of some physiological discomfort or ill health. On the other hand, we see that the body is always on the slide toward entropy and decay.

∗∗∗

Next, we are introduced to the theme of the Feminine for the first time. It is no secret that men famously misunderstand women, considering them alien creatures with alien needs and desires. What do women want, really? As men we are almost always at a loss to explain their behaviors and understand their motivations. The greatest irony of a man's life is that a woman is both necessary to his fulfillment, and simultaneously the source of endless misgivings. Even the most self-assured man can be turned upside down by insecurities a woman inspires and draws out of him. With woman, he is always on shifting ground.

It is instructive that Henson turned his only significant female character into a pig. Nietzsche equated the Feminine with irrationality, as opposed to male rationality. It was a man's task to reign in and shape the irrational energies of the libido, and the irrational part of himself, and use the feminine creative energy inside himself. But one had to be careful—it was easy to get swallowed by the irrational, and lose one's mind. Just as, in real life, it is easy to get swallowed by a woman. If a man is unable to draw lines in a relationship (especially these days), he will be consumed by his spouse or partner. Once a woman finds the man she wants, she will go about dismantling him into bite-sized bits. Over the years, he will realize he has no idea who he is, and is out of touch with the person he was so many years ago.

This is a theme that continuously comes into play in the film; the relationship between the Feminine and Masculine. The issue will be discussed later in the film, but we see the Military Eagle whipping his cadre of hens into shape. This suggests virility, as he seems able to please all these lady hens. Again, the insinuation is that America has that combination of youthfulness and vitality necessary to propel us into the future, by utilizing the feminine, but by dominating its procreative energies with a Masculine will to power.

The all male ensemble of the Muppets means that Miss Piggy alone is the representative of the Feminine. Modern mankind is in a shambles, a democratic din of competing drives that hardly seem capable of unification. Miss Piggy is in a mud mask, staring at herself in the mirror. Her hair is washed. Clearly she is sequestered, looking freshly showered and toweled, there is no doubt that she does not need to wrestle with the others for space in the bathroom. She has her own quarters.

Immediately after Miss Piggy's choosing of outfits, none which seems to suit her, we see two aged men on the seat outside her room. Neither is the palsied old man who passed by Kermit's room earlier. These are two different elderly males, good friends. They are older, and seem like twins. They are comfortable. They are outside the ruckus of younger men's competing drives and torn psyches. They have merged into a unified being. They wear robes similar to Kermit's. Kermit is old enough now that he would like to join them, but for now he has a household to maintain.

They seem to be yawning at the peek inside Miss Piggy's room, the realm of feminine mysteries. They have seen into the feminine world, and are no longer intrigued or aroused by it. They are looking at a half-naked woman (even if she is a pig), but could care less. They are apart from the melee of competing elements, restful and yawning. They have become quiet and at peace. We will not see them again in this film, for this story is still about the young, who still remain in the fight. It is thus in the younger male that we seek the kind of Masculinity that will be of use to use. A Masculinity for which the Feminine is still a mystery to be explored and conquered.

Then we see Kermit in line for the bathroom, tapping his feet both to the music and also what seems impatience. He is waiting for the two Cosmic Fish in the toilet to get done with their washing. They are not the Cosmic Fish yet, however. Fish are historically symbolic of the vagina. There are two, because each represents an egg of the female.

A third fish, more phallic in aspect, then bites on the toilet paper and approaches the two fish in the toilet. He seems like a penis approaching them with some kind of mating dance. But why does he bring toilet paper? It is white and long, and immediately reminds us of ejaculation. But if he is ejaculating towards these fish, why is toilet paper used? TP is also used to clean, and the suggestion is that it is only with the male seed, the Masculine, that the Feminine can cease to be a merely sexualized object. Fertility is the true fulfillment of female and male promise.

∗∗∗

In a film so densely layered as this, there are often up to four or five themes operating simultaneously in any given frame. That said, while we recognize the collegiality of the Muppets in their tightly-packed domicile, we also bear witness to the tensions naturally created by this level of population density. With possibly a dozen or more bedrooms but apparently only one bathroom, each Muppet struggles to find the personal space to bathe, cleanse, and otherwise perform their morning ablutions. This competition for available resources mirrors our own, wherein we vie with one another for access to a finite availability of material wealth and comfort.

Animal, that vessel of all things beastly and the very embodiment of appetite, leaves his bedroom and jumps into the morning melee. Not so chipper at this bright hour, he displays his contempt by aggressively shouldering his way past those in line into the bathroom. Nobody makes a peep as he demonstrates master morality, acting well outside the bounds of aristocratic restraint.

Immediately after we see the chef making breakfast in the kitchen. He is cracking an egg, the very sign of life (and certainly in this film), into a bowl. This marks a series of quick cut scenes calling back to one another in rapid succession. Animal is trying to find somewhere to clean himself, a desire to purify and neuter his libidinal spirit in a quest to become something more than a mere animal and beast.

Alas, he is still willing to be dirty, as when he cannot find a place to wash, he dunks his head in the toilet. This scatological suggestion shows that there is still something primal inside himself that will not easy be washed away, even when he is making every attempt to "get clean." Then we cut to the cook again. He is kneading dough into a phallic shape. The bread will rise, like invigorated cocks. The suggestion here is that Animal still has some lust inside him, and a libidinal urge. In the next scene we are shown the gathering of Muppets at the breakfast table, all chair-dancing to the music. Coffee in hand, they are stimulated, awoken, and have risen back to life. Yet it is the assertion of their natural rigor, not the artificial stimulant of caffeine, that is giving them their lust for life. They are experiencing the reawaking of internal passions, which have been put to sleep in the older members of the household. As Nietzsche said, blessed are the sleepy, for they shall soon nod off.

He is the will to power, the very source of the will to power in ourselves. How does the will to power function in our economy?

After finding no room at the sink he pulls the shower curtain back on a clutch of washing hens. The bathtub is a gathering of groundlings. Turned about, he is forced to perform his morning hygiene in the toilet. He dunks his head and flushes, the swirling waters acting as a cleansing shower. And though Animal appears to come clean, it is suggested that in our real world struggle for assets, many of us will at last find ourselves rooting around in unclean territory.

This, friends, is the very Rat Race. There is a finite amount of riches, and we are born into a giant brawl for the available lucre. Though it's false to say there is a fixed amount of wealth, the statement is true in a practical sense. Wealth is constantly being created. Indeed, the goal of capitalist societies is to always be increasing the amount of wealth for every member. Yet in terms of our own lives, we seem to always be in competition for what appears a limited cache. Every dollar not in your pocket goes to someone other schlub, and this seems unreasonable.

So we start businesses, earn degrees, vie for promotions and salary increases, search for tax write-offs, and so on. In this way we can purchase increasingly conspicuous signifiers of our financial acuity, and announce our economic virility to peers. But the competition never ceases, and we must forever run the treadmill, chasing a carrot at the end of a stick. All this goes on against the backdrop we have been discussing. The real tragedy of the Rat Race is not that it puts us on a never-ending path of materialism, but rather, that this Race goes on as if in defiant opposition of the dark truth encroaching on us.

It is not my intention to cast aspersions on this preoccupation with accumulating wealth. Nor, do I believe, is it the aim of *Muppets From Space*. As we already mentioned, the drive for wealth creates excess, which those more disposed to spiritual pursuits can feed off of. To paraphrase Jesus, this segment in the film is for those who have ears to hear it. A certain type of person, the seeker, will find this all-consuming pursuit of wealth disagreeable. They want to invest their talents and energies elsewhere, and believe they have something different to contribute. These souls understand that by throwing themselves into the ring, by participating in the rat race, they would deprive the world of something quite valuable—something only they can offer. This may be equally delusional; sadly, not all who opt out of the materialistic mania will discover a deeper and truer happiness. As often as not, a resentment builds not only towards those who have stayed true to the blind chase of acquisition, but towards existence, which failed to provide the promised succor of a life less ordinary.

Along these lines, to deny the chase for comfort and riches as life's primary focus can induce a bad conscience. As in questioning the existence of God, we find ourselves going against the grain of our fellows. At the very moment we doubt, we become strangers in our own tribe. Certain philosophers have even suggested that denying the drive for amassing wealth is contrary to life, as life is most of all a pursuit for self-embellishment. The average person knows this drive primarily through acquisition and worldly accolades. This bad conscience becomes even more acute if we find ourselves living in poverty and insecurity. We must ward off our own accusatory voice, which brands us a failure. Sadly, these are often the consequences of following our dreams.

But we must remember that we are replaceable in the world of work. If not us, some other warm body will do the task we supposed ourselves essential to. There may be something only we are capable of, and it is this we need to discover.

Because we only have so much time, energy, and force of will, we must practice a strict personal economics if we are to become what we're meant to become. We must invest our time cautiously and consciously. A myth common to our age is that we can be all things. That each of our various longings can be fulfilled. It's a powerful delusion, and persists even into our old age, until that sad day when we realize the opportunity to chase down every last one of our dreams has come and gone. There is no more time, and certain doors are closed to us forever. And while there is a positive and enriching element to this myth, it can also be destructive.

On the bright side, believing an array of options will always be open to us can inspire us to reorient ourselves. Even very late in life we can opt to live according to a variety of value systems. But this openness can also lead us to waste a great deal of years living lives that never suited us to begin with, because we feel there is ample time to correct our course. But there is never enough time for all things.

***

We find Kermit gathering with the entire household in the living room. In sync, the massive crew gleefully dances out the last few bars of the funk anthem "Brick House." The song breaks off sharp after a rousing crescendo. A group catharsis is achieved in a ritual way, spirits communally lifted and released. The gang breaks up, each to meet their day's demands. As they depart, Kermit looks approvingly over his brood and says, "Way to get down with your bad selves." Though probably long dated by now, this slang term so familiar to the 1990's—when taken with a degree of literalness—transcends the decade it belongs to, and becomes a universal approval of what is called "evil" in humankind. Why does Kermit, here in the very room that is synonymous with "living," approve of his brood's indulgence in their evil instincts?

We return, as we often will, to Nietzsche, who famously offered an assessment of good and evil that turned traditional prejudice on its head. Scandalizing his more prudent contemporaries, Nietzsche argued that what we call evil is a conveniently flexible term for certain instincts, which at times might be crucial to the health and survival of an individual and even a species. The idea that evil is wholly to be avoided is ignorant. When we spiritualize certain emotions, they can be empowering.

Those instincts we call good are the herd instincts. Sharing, giving, self-sacrificie and so on. Those instincts called evil—violence, jealousy, hatred—are precisely those called upon

But regardless, it is an interesting choice of words, and leads us to a meditation on Good and Evil, Good and Bad.

Kermit is exposed here as a character of fascinating contradictions. While Gonzo's own torments of the soul are the film's focus, we must remember to take second and third looks at the characters surrounding him. Gonzo's sickness is universal to modern man, and cannot be understood apart from his social context. An ensemble cast must still have a lead, but supporting players must be used to unpack and interpret the protagonist's narrative arc.

Kermit is a broken-down man, stoop-shouldered and domesticated. A deep, debilitating fatigue spills from his eyes, and his poor posture hints at a worn-down, world-weary soul. Hardly the kind of beast we would expect to find promoting evil instincts, we can see that what he is approving in others is the thing that has long ago died inside himself. And what has died? The spark of exuberant life; the rakish and mischievous face flashed against the withering world like a shield; all the bravado of youth and vitality and courage. All these signs of life—of audacious, vigorous, and lusty life—are gone. Here lies Kermit the Frog, his own body an ambulatory tomb for his decomposing spirit. Kermit the Shambles, Kermit the Dry Husk.

Just look at how Kermit praises the evil demonstrated by his brood. Still able to recognize in others what he can no longer indulge in, he is delighted they still have the capacity for evil. Yet it was only a half-hearted endorsement, apathetically delivered. This is not to say the sentiment was disingenuous, only that Kermit's wane praise is a blessing bestowed by a neutered soul, haunted by its own tame domesticity. His sanction has no blood, and is inspired by allegiance to an ideal he shares no part in. The pitiable frogman merely pays lip service to a shriveled mode of being he must have believed in at one time. Knowing his praise is partly a sham, he at least has the decency to downplay his enthusiasm, lest he become a false priest and prophet, charlatan and sham to the very people who put faith in his leadership, wisdom and authenticity. If the authentic state of things is lackluster and uninspired, at least he was honorable toward that truth.

Kermit's own spiritual malaise—different from Gonzo's but branching from the same diseased root—is exposed by the fact his bedroom décor is a simulacrum of the very swamps and lakebeds his ancestors lived, loved, killed and were killed in. His four walls have become a harmless, Disnified homage to the red-clawed, sharp-toothed environment of his froggy forebears. These green fiends trounced around in a swamp, yes—they slept outdoors and rooted around in sludge—but how gloriously *alive* they were! Each precious second of their days was spent answering directly to nature's call. They slept when tired, ate when hungry, roamed where they pleased, and mated with filthy and furious abandon beneath the pale beaming torch of the full moon, under the ecstatically approving gaze of the goddess Luna.

There in the murky muck and untamed wilds, each organism was able to fully express itself to the bounds of its genetic limits. Allowed—nay, forced—to become the best beast they could possibly become. They were as fast as they could be, as alert, as lucid, as savage and barbarous as the circumstances called for; or alternately, as kind and compassionate. They were attuned to their environment, constantly reacting to invigorating stimuli and whatever surprise came roaring from the reeds—they didn't shuffle through their world like a ghost or a zombie. They were equally in tune with their physical bodies, knowing the limits of their prowess, but knowing just as well those limits could be broken. The body could be counted on once again to perform when it counted most, and against insurmountable odds—the body was everything, wherein God and his creation were in unified communion.

Above all, this was a life lived in the flesh—not a half-felt slog through soul-grinding duties and hallucinatory tedium. Outbursts of real emotion were tied to matters of real consequence, and were not a thin spew of sound and fury, signifying nothing, set against a backdrop of strip malls, Internet memes, office buildings, quarterly reports, intramural soccer leagues and must-see-TV. Passion has already become parody in our watered-down, media-saturated world. When we speechify or take a stand, or when others do, the inspirational theme music from certain films or television shows automatically cues up at the back of our minds.

Our entire existence, it seems, has become mostly an imitation of existence—our lives feel like dress rehearsals for a production that will never be staged. Or in modern parlance, a TV show that was never meant to air (or in contemporary parlance, a YouTube video that found no viewer clicks—no, not even one, and nor would it ever). We become more cerebral but less profound. By doing so, we have swapped sensuality for mental approximations of sensuality ; we have opted to inhabit imaginary worlds—wondrous and magical, bounded only by the limits of our own creativity—that have no consequence or weight.

When that body could not respond—when it was too old or injured or outmatched—death came with speed and drama. None died in silent isolation after endless years wasting away and growing alienated from the active world. The placid and peaceful shores of a pond may bring idyllic thoughts to our own minds, but make no mistake, the place is a jungle where the triumphs and failures, agonies and ecstasies, are all lived on a scale equal to the grandest—their tragedies, too, echo through the halls of eternity.

How telling that Kermit lives in a cartoon version of his beloved wilds! His boudoir is constructed entirely as an escape from his wearying domestic life. No doubt when he slips into his sheets at night his mind travels far, far away. He goes hopping madly through the grass. Eyeballing a juicy fly, camouflaging himself among the reeds to snap out his tongue and hurl his trophy down his throat! To plunge into the water and swim, the golden rays of the sun bursting gently overhead. To feel the limbs work and the blood pump! To fight with other frogs for breeding rights and the amorous attentions of the female! To feel oneself at one with one's own life, not a mere tangent to it, not a mere ghost with a thirty year mortgage and an office job. And this is the man who praises evil! A man who nightly dreams of it!

Relatedly, a society born of blood and struggle that later grows pudgy and comfortable—soft around the middle and lenient towards itself—will still be worshipful of its heroic past. Wars and revolutions call out the beast in us, the vital instincts are all engaged, and we seem far more alive than in times of peace. Having built our sad, limp lives on the backs of our ancestors' glorious and epic struggles, we are ashamed to look in the mirror, and grab at our love handles while asking ourselves what we've become. The lives we lead do not require heroism or adventure—ours are banal lives of repetitive maintenance and dull responsibilities, all in service to creature comforts and inane little indulgences of pleasure. As we come to recognize our own descent into sedentary, sedate contentment—when we tally all the sacrifices we've made to the Gods of Convenience—the more embarrassing our inauthentic praises to animal vitality become. Our reverence to our forebears becomes pathetically hollow, kneeling as we are before the gravestones of our dead ideals.

As Nietzsche said, go to any zoo and behold the tamed animal, and then see that same species in the wilds—can you say the tamed species has been improved by his incarceration? Hardly. And yet is the same with the tiger as it is with the human being. Modern civilization, for all its history of barbarity, is for the great majority of us a prison where we are castrated and broken. If we could but see our society in its naked framework, we would see that we are but breeders for a system that has gotten out of our control and now moves only according to its own momentum. It is the animal still capable of evil that thrives.

***

Kermit's sad schlep through the blurring, recurring doldrums of daily life is a disheartening mimicry of our own. It's hard not to identify with the big, green goofball. Are our own pathetic run-of-the-mill lives any different from his? We are the frog who stands dumbstruck from time to time, as if a brick has just been blasted against our head, clearing the fog and letting us see things clearly as they are. Both stupefied and terribly lucid, we ask ourselves: "Is this all there is?" We have traded adventure for security and spontaneity for stability. Look at that crushed, literally stoop-shouldered bastard! Methinks there is a part of him in all of us. Perhaps there are those in our midst whose everyday life is a non-stop thrill ride, . But no doubt the great majority of us are living lives of quiet desperation.

First, and rather significantly, Kermit approaches the dining table where he will join the others for the morning repast. He enters from the left, and at the same time, from the right of the screen, a smaller and younger version of himself walks towards him. Though technically Kermit's nephew Robin, the casual Muppet viewer has no knowledge of this, and it seems to us that Kermit the man and Kermit the child are walking towards his seat at the head of the table from opposite ends.

Almost in the same manner that Kermit willfully ignored the old man stumbling past him as the specter of old age, he now looks over his youthful self with a sad bemusement. His sorrow is in his eyes and the hang of his head, and while he drinks in the specter of his own youthfulness, he is also detached. To ponder over the passage of time, and the disparities between the adults we are and the adults we hoped to be when we were young, is altogether too depressing. It would sink many of us into the depths, from which we might never arise. Young Kermit looks down here, as if to avert eyes with his older self. It's a painfully touching moment.

There is certainly an element of disapproval in Middle-Age Kermit's look, and at first it seems like this is why Young Kermit lowers his gaze. MA Kermit stares at the boy he was, and can't believe how ignorant and idealistic he was. He thought life would be full of romance and adventure, and that there was no limit of options and choices and chances to change. It is with both longing and loathing he sees himself. And it is also defensive in part, for even though Young Kermit says nothing, Old Kermit is ashamed and trying not to be ashamed. It's as if Young Kermit is an accusation Old Kermit must assault. No, I haven't lived up to my promise! But I had responsibilities! Bills to pay!

And while chastised, it may indeed be as much from shame at the man he became—the child always the father of the man—at the scolding eyes. We can opt for domesticity or something truly revolutionary. How many sacrifices have their been to the God of domesticity? Nephew asks Kermit what he is going to do with his vacation. Kermit had been hoping to do nothing but relax, and lose himself in the domestic chores that now seem to define him. While this may be his hope though, events will soon unfold that will pull him rudely away from his domestic routine.

We have been introduced to the feminine once, when we saw Miss Piggy in her bedroom going through the machinations of her toilet. Our second introduction is when Miss Piggy slams through the dining room door in some showy garment, ready for her big day at work. She smashes the door against a servant rabbit carrying a creamy cake. He is flung hard against the wall as she marches past without notice. The door swings closed and we see the rabbit pinned up against the wall, covered in thick, white goop. He falls forward onto the ground, dead or unconscious.

This is the second time we have are introduced to an Onanistic theme, and seed being "wasted on the ground." The rabbit is most particularly famous as a symbol for unbridled breeding and procreative regeneration. And here the female of the house has rendered him impotent, the dripping cream covering his body like semen spilled from a withdrawing penis on the face, hair and chest. We see this motif often enough in pornography, the medium which most revels in the sex act divorced from its biological intent. Is this an accusation against

History has done strange things with the feminine mystique, and today the modern woman stands out as distinct from her forebears in most every way possible. For decades the most poignant conversation women have had with themselves is how to have it all; most particularly how to have both a family and career, without either falling short of the ideal, and neither being sacrificed to the other. It is a profound dilemma the modern family faces, especially as we are stretched thin and burdened by debt. We are running on a treadmill, after a carrot on a stick, and it is said that these days we are no longer even offered a carrot. We are the mules of the economic engine, working ourselves threadbare and to exhaustion, earning our middle class stripes while making those who truly control America wealthier and wealthier.

And while we may live in a time that our children most require a close familial bond, and particularly with the mother, she is forced to enter the work force or is inclined to by some sense that a career will justify her existence. This is another expose of the domestic life as both a place of gathering and a trap, an ironically sterile realm where the female is infertile. We are given to understand the contemporary woman is also expending her libidinal energies as wastefully as her spouse. What is the modern domestic routine? Is it the foundation from which we grow into ourselves, or the stage in which we grow away from ourselves? *Muppets From Space* may not have the answers, but it certainly goes about begging the question.

***

As the Muppets sit down to enjoy their morning repast the oven explodes, ending the exuberance of the communal meal before it has even begun. Maintaining a household is a constant struggle against natural entropy. Things fall apart, and it often feels like the greatest store of our energies is spent just holding everything together. Domestic concerns become perpetual, day-to-day, until at last they themselves become the entire purpose of our lives. While in theory a house in good order is a steppingstone to self-actualization, in reality it tends to sap our energies for more uplifting endeavors. There are those people who take great pleasure in orchestrating the dynamics of the home, and there is no cause for alarm in this.

The mind reels at just how busied we are by the inanities of adult life. How on earth do we stay atop this landslide of chores? The laundry is always piling up, as is the ironing—and then the clothes must be folded and put away. Meals have to be planned, groceries have to be gotten, and dinners have to be prepared. The meals should be healthy, and we have to make important choices where we shop and what we buy. We should buy organic, because pesticides, preservatives, and flavorings in many foods is toxic to us. But we must also research the food we eat, and be skeptical of certain foods claiming to be organic when they are not. We must research what the qualifications are to be certified organic, and then decide which products are doing more than meeting the minimal definition. We should also think about where our meat comes from. We don't want the animals we consume to be raised and slaughtered under inhumane conditions. We should only buy free range eggs, but we need to also be aware that the definition of free range may not be what we think it is. Free range may simply mean that the cages for the chickens are large enough to turn around in, not that they roam free and gay in an open air pen, as if on some small family farm. Our meals should also be tasty, so we should do our best to improve our cooking skills.

There are bills to be paid: water, sewage, electricity, and gas. We must pay attention to our utility usage—we have to keep the bills as low as possible. Energy efficiency is good for our pocketbooks, but we also must consider our impact on the Earth's environment. We need to sort our trash and recycle, to reduce our waste—and we should also compost. This compost can be tended to so that it is good soil for the small gardens we should be growing, as that way we know where our vegetables are coming from. It also puts us in touch with the Earth and our own diets, which we've grown accustomed to not thinking much about. The plants must be watered, the flowers dead-headed, the bushes kept tidy. The yard must be attended to, and for that tools will need to be purchased. At the very least a lawnmower. Some of us can hire people to care for our lawns, and these must be budgeted for.

We must make the house payment. Also, we need insurance for fire or some other disaster—and we must also be covered for burglary. We should review our policy and know which policy is best for our needs. We must also have at least one car, if not more. And there needs to be insurance on these cars, and we should know which insurance policy is best for our needs—liability? Full coverage? We should also pay attention to what our warranty says about maintenance on our vehicles—some services are offered free from the dealership, and some aspects of our warranty may be voided if we don't keep to the vehicle's maintenance schedule. We need to pay attention to our mileage so that we know when certain parts must be replaced or certain services provided. We should also pay attention to our tires, because driving on bad tires can be very dangerous.

We should have life insurance, health insurance, and dental insurance—we need to have the right plan for our needs, and compare our plans with other plans. We might be paying too much, or even too little. Our plan may not cover certain things that should be covered, and may cover certain things we don't really need covered. We should also get regular teeth cleanings and screenings for a host of different diseases—

cancer, diabetes, thyroid disorders, and so on. We should also have a retirement plan, and research that plan to see if it is the one that most suits our needs. It wouldn't hurt to have burial insurance either, as funerals can be very expensive and leave loved ones in a great deal of debt. We also need a will, and that will needs to be amended from time to time, as our assets grow or circumstances of our lives change. And through this all we should also remain to retain a robust savings account, because life often has surprises in store for us, such as the loss of a job, an illness, or a relocation to a new city. But we also need to be aware that not all savings plans are equal, and many offer interest rates and other growth incentives. Still, most savings accounts don't really do much, and you should research other options on how to make your money work for you. Remember to do all the relevant research though, as some investment plans may not be those most suited to your needs.

Exactly when is this insanity supposed to stop? Keeping up with these demands not only takes up our free time, but lades whatever freedom we have left with worry, anxiety and stress. The dailies of life leech off psychic energy, because not only must we attend to all these regular duties, we must also keep a record of how we've attended to these duties, either in writing or in our minds. Can we never have peace from all these mundane concerns? Must they sap us until that longed-for day when the Reaper comes calling? The merry-go-round is never supposed to stop, and once we are on it extracting ourselves from the web becomes harder with each passing year. We are buried beneath this avalanche of banal obligations, and we are suffocating. With fading breath, we demand an answer to the question: *Is this all there is?*

As patriarch of the household, Kermit the Frog is burdened with its upkeep. The viewer can easily see that this frog feels "put upon" by his duties, that all this exasperating busywork has left him broken in every way. In almost every scene there is a point when he lets off a deflated sigh, and his slumped shoulders seem like a physical symptom of his oppression. As Thoreau famously said, "We do not own a house, a house owns us." As adults we must all accept that domestic duties will consume a great deal of our time on Earth. An ordered house is indeed a blessing, this we can acknowledge. However we must also recognize that domestic duties put us constantly at risk of losing sight of higher callings. Mundane concerns will bury us under an avalanche of banality, and it is this that the spiritual among us must rebel against.

Later in the film we'll see several main characters gathered around a card table, playing poker. Instead of money the characters throw prized belongings into the pot. We are being told that the life of domesticity is nothing if not a gamble, and that it isn't money which is truly at stake. And if not money, then what do we ante? All those things about human life that are precious, magical, and inspire awe. We gamble away our hopes and dreams by storing up nuts and delaying gratification. By living responsibly. But we lose the gamble when circumstances take an unforeseen twist—as is said, life is what happens to you when you're making other plans. We might come down with cancer or heart disease, or be injured in an accident. The pensions we spent years investing in may disappear in the blink of an eye through the greedy machinations of financial investors. The houses we spent so much time and energy turning into homes may be just a few payments away from being lost forever, if we should lose our jobs in a bad economy. There is no security these days, and we all stand on thin ice. This anxiety is killing us.

And in the midst of all this insecurity, there is the one thing that is supposed to sustain us through it all: Love. But does anybody believe in this kind of love any more? Science has done away with our romantic understanding of love, and we see it for the bio-chemical hormonal process it is. It comes over us in a burst of infatuation, and fizzles out into a tenuous tolerance. With more than half of all marriages ending in divorce, and those that survive looking less than ideal, more and more people opt not to participate in the institution. We see that love grows strained, and tenuously predicated on certain promises that many of us will be unable to keep over the long haul. With the ideal of a permanent and lasting home having dissolved, so too does our idea of somebody with whom we can share it. Many of us expect marriage to ensure a particular lifestyle and quality of living—if this should fail to materialize, the so-called love upon which the arrangement was predicated may seem like a flimsy foundation after all.

Lastly, having children may seem like a bulwark against purposelessness. And though their existence in our lives may seem to be a bulwark against purposelessness, we can no more count on them than anything else. Children disappoint us, or grow estranged—or we as parents disappoint and fail them. At long last the unbreakable bond of family ties grows thin and dry before snapping completely. Our real fear, growing old and feeble and alone, happens regardless of how much we've devoted ourselves to our children. Children, busy with their own lives, must at last abandon their fathers and mothers to the cold, institutional hands of assisted living and old folks homes. They may even feel resentful, and they may feel guilty, that by giving them existence we have simply doomed them to repeat the jog on the same soul-sucking treadmill that we have, and thereby perpetuating the whole sad spectacle for our own selfish reasons.

***

After the failed effort at a group feast, there is an event implicating Gonzo as a young Jewish male, though his ethnicity of course remains mysterious. Indeed, he cannot literally be Jewish, even within the magical realist world of the Muppets, for we later learn that he is not of this Earth. Even if the psychology of Jews were unfamiliar to us, it would take a very hardened heart to declare that Jews are aliens among us. Many Jews would take offense, and considering the centuries of bias against them, it's probably in poor taste.

Though as gentiles we can never enter fully into the mind of a Jew, we should presume their emotive and mental processes occur much as ours do; for as Shakespeare asked, If you prick the Jew, does he not bleed? Aye, he has hands, organs, and dimensions, harmed and healed by the same means as you and I. For this film, you might replace Jew with alien, and thereby conclude that being an extraterrestrial by no means disqualifies Gonzo from the sting of discontents that plague mankind in general. All sentient species must surely have, at one time or another in their spiritual evolution, been weighted down with ruminations on the death of God, in whatever form theirs took. From the Milky Way to

MACS0647—at over thirteen billion light away, the furthest galaxy from Earth—things are no doubt much the same in this department.

On this particular morning Gonzo has decided to abstain from work, declining to participate in the banal routine of daily life. Sensing that somehow enlightenment can only reach him when he is not otherwise occupied, he knows he must temporarily step away. For one day at least, he is unshackled from grinding economic motives. His line of work is as a performer, shot from a cannon in finale to some sparkly variety show. It is theatrical and vaudevillian, a true circus. Of course he would be employed as an entertainer! His very life is a stage production, far from authenticity and the *real*. Entertaining a group who are only actors at life themselves puts Gonzo at an even further remove from what can genuinely be called life. He is a dancing clown, a monkey, performing for a pittance: the empty and ephemeral approval of the audience. Before a crowd, as in life, he presents a thin, unthreatening caricature of himself to a world that denies him a deeper sense of self, a rich inner life, or complicated personality. He is a tool, exploited as a means, an alienated laborer in a sparkly Rhine-stoned leotard.

On this day Gonzo has been scheduled to perform at a bar mitzvah, a Jewish boy's inauguration into manhood. After the Hebraic imagery of the opening dream-sequence, this thematic echo should not be taken lightly, as if it were coincidental dross. Gonzo could have been scheduled to perform at any number of events, but none would have packed the narrative punch of this ancient celebration. In symbolic terms, it is Gonzo who is to be the initiate at this rite. To be shot out of a cannon is to fly through the air and go great distances, advancing forward in one bound at a velocity impossible to the step-by-step cadence of bipedal locomotion. Only birds share this privilege, and it has always been man's dream to flap the wings of freedom and soar away from his milieu. But in this case, it is intended that Gonzo carry the baggage of the past in his flight, and to soar only within the confines of a very specific script.

Rites of initiation exist in every culture, and those celebrating the transition from childhood to adulthood are known as puberty rites. Among these are baptism, Confirmation, and an entire slew of tribal and native ceremonies. By enacting the pageantry of these inherited rituals, the youth becomes an accepted member of the tribe, expected to participate as an adult, aping the morals, values, and ethnic identity that is his inheritance. We must remember that Christianity is only a splinter sect of Judaism, uncannily adopted by the whole of Western civilization. It remains at bottom a Jewish spiritual paradigm. By denying himself entry through the magical means of the bar mitzvah, Gonzo is rejecting the whole of Judeo-Christian teachings; both its morality and worldview. He won't fly far in the Jewish tradition—just as rightly said, the Judeo-Christian tradition—and calls all of it into question—no longer accepting its answer to the question of mankind's place in the universe.

Faced with the gloom of reality, we often choose ready answers to hard questions. An answer that we suspect may be false, but which offers relief from our doubts. But perhaps if we are willing to feel lost, abandoned, or depressed for a little longer, a different answer may present itself to us. Perhaps the beauty is in the searching, and not the finding. Offered an impermeable creed and entry into a community of like-minded believers, Gonzo chooses exile. He'd rather live despondently than falsely. This should not be seeing as a merely negative action, though. In rejecting the Judeo-Christian, Gonzo has set himself up to experience a more mature relationship to existence. He will plumb his despair to the depths, searching for whatever nugget of wisdom lay lost in the bottommost muck.

Gonzo is holding out for a deeper connection. It is not his own coming of age he thirsts for, but mankind's own, a mature and knowing relationship to the cosmos, free from the fog of ancient ideologies. He may come to recognize the universe as a profoundly atheistic place, with no reverence for—or even awareness of—the petty aspirations of man. But a new spiritual approach cannot be nurtured into being without killing off old paradigms, or by ignoring the latest scientific knowledge about the natural world.

**

It is Gonzo's good fortune that even on such short notice another crew is willing to fill in for him at the Bar Mitzvah. These others will bring the acrobatic theatricality that is the gold standard of Gonzo the Great. Perhaps Gonzo will be missed, and then again, perhaps not. It's a fine lesson, if a sharp one, that we should all learn. As individualistic as we may be, or as we in fact are, it takes only a modicum of effort to replace us. So many of us believe that we are essential at the workplace. Rest assured, we are not. Perhaps out of our slavish devotion to work, we convince ourselves that things would fall apart were we not there to keep it all together. Recognizing our dispensability is one of the first steps towards enlightenment. We are superfluous; and finding that thing which ONLY we are capable of is probably a precursor to wholeness. I say probably because there is never a guarantee of wholeness, regardless of whether or not we are "necessary."

In fact, how much less necessary are we to the human race than to our job? It is only to the family that we are part of that we become necessary beings.

As the substitute troupe hauls their equipment out the door, we see they are dressed in gaudy, sequined, Rhinestone-covered costumes. This fashion is oft associated with trapeze artists, Liberace, and Elvis impersonators specializing in the crooner's obese, drug-addled years. Clearly *some* kind of circus is planned, and the smart money is on a crass extravaganza. This coming of age will have little or no solemnity. Is this what the bar mitzvah has become in our day and age? A cheap imitation or parody of itself? One wonders, yes. And the more one wonders, one begins to suspect the answer is firmly in the Yes camp. Our rituals and rites have become so bloated, fragmented, and disconnected from their original intentions that they are all of them parodies. They are all contextual, and none has universal appeal or meaning aside from their meaning to the individual person being celebrated.

The Bar Mitzvah itself seems like a cheap imitation or parody of its former self. Of course, the Bar Mitzvahs as a spiritual event is famously corrupted. I myself have been in attendance at the Bar Mitvahs, and was stunned at the grossly materialistic overtones and unabashedly garish festivities.

Gonzo, who seeks an initiation into a true spiritual existence will not make do with such a mockery of the sacred: the mock sacred.

It would be remiss here to not discuss Jewish otherness. In this day and age it is to court offense when we discuss the Jews as an "other." This should come as no surprise. Not only are Jews in America very well assimilated, but America as a nation is flexible enough to absorb every ethnic identity into a blurred American character. The move of so many minorities to carve out an ethnic identity is in fact counter to the American spirit. As many theorists point out, America was not founded upon familial lines, but instead under the umbrella of political and philosophical ideas. That said, Jews have in part been stigmatized throughout history as the alien in the midst. As a general thing, Jewish people are perhaps most famous for their unwillingness to be absorbed into the more powerful societies that happen to govern them. They have been reviled in part due to their refusal to interbreed and accept the gods, practices, and norms of the civilization who ruled over them. This always created suspicion against them.

Nietzsche has it that this isolation is what turned the Jews into a moralizing people. By moralizing, I mean a people that was capable of putting forth an ethic as a people.

After saying that Electric Mayhem has taken over for him. The scene in question begins with Gonzo describing his depression to Kermit. The other Muppets have left the house, attending to their various goings-on. Gonzo doesn't want to go to work because he is too deeply saddened by his own ignorance concerning his origins and role in the world. The bubble of his day-to-day life has been punctured by the sharp edges of intensely philosophical questions. He approaches Kermit seeking advice and comfort. He earnestly lays out his fears about his role in the world. In short, Gonzo is lonesome, and feels that life is happening to him.He has not been able to impose himself on the world. Tired of being a one of a kind freak, Gonzo cannot will his own meaning.

Though sympathetic, our dear frog lead is distracted. Kermit is far too busy to lend a true ear to Gonzo's concerns. The pull of practical life is hard, and sucks Kermit in like an eddy. As Kermit attentively sits, intending to offer fatherly wisdom to Gonzo, the pair are interrupted by news that the house painters have arrived, and that they are headed down the street because Animal bit one (the animal rages against the duties of the home). They need instruction, these house painters. Kermit runs after them, saying "Wait guys, he's just a musician." Nietzsche association with music.

As with Kermit, so too with us. The so-called realities of life pull us further away from spiritual pondering, and not too many years go by before we lose our hunger for the answers. Our senses become dulled, and we mope through life, heaped upon by daily duties. The question is, what is real life? Is real life attendance to these mundane concerns that daily draw us farther away from the real purpose of our lives.

In this moment we are given further confirmation that these Muppets exist in a world in which God has died. That the film accepts this premise is evidenced by God's conspicuous absence from any discussion of meaning. When the depth of Gonzo's existential crisis is recognized by Kermit, the most natural direction to steer him in would presumably be towards religious faith, which acts as a balm for so many souls bearing the weight of modern secularism. But nobody thinks to mention God in this film, as if the very idea of Him had never existed. He is removed from all discussions of purpose, and nobody advances the position that through Him transcendence can be achieved. It is presumed that the pleasures of life will be enough to sate the soul, and that camaraderie is itself sufficient to quiet any yearnings for transcendence.

It is worthwhile here—nay, essential—to discuss the myth of the Eternal Jew, or Wandering Jew. More accurately, the Eternally Wandering Jew. He goes hither and tither, with no release from his nomadic rambles; for these rambles are his unique curse.

For those ignorant of the concept, the Eternal Jew arises out of medieval folklore, but has its roots in the Bible. Legend has it that a Jew who mocked Jesus was condemned to roam the Earth until Christ's second coming.

However, several Jewish writers themselves have appropriated the concept, transferring the Beginning during the events narrated in the Book of Exodus, this cultural meme is thought to continue living within the psyches of the Jewish Diaspora, for whom Israel, or some metaphorical equivalent, is the sought-after home. Gonzo's Israel is of the metaphorical kind. He seeks a family in the Family of Man, a place of profound belonging.

After Gonzo lays out his concerns to Kermit, Kermit goes chasing after the house painters. After the infamous breakfast scene in which Kermit describes Gonzo as "distinct," rather than hopelessly "estranged from his fellows," as Gonzo sees it, the film cuts to lovingly framed photographs of various Muppet characters side-by-side with their friends and loved ones. It seems every Muppet besides Gonzo belongs to a family, whether biological or fraternal; all but him have somebody to hold and be unconditionally loved by. Beaker, their man of science, has Doctor Honeydew, Fozzie has his "beary" loving family, and Kermit of course has Miss Piggy. After panning slowly over all these images of smiles and happy times shared with loved ones, we come to Gonzo's portrait. It is the perfect picture of alienation and despair. He stands as a far-off figure upon the sands of a deserted beach, the weather cloudy and full of portentous gloom. He is transfixed before the shoreline staring into the dark mystery of the turbulent ocean.

The expression on Gonzo's face is such that he seems to be peering into infinite sadness. The tragedy that is life and death has crept upon him like a wave and finally washed over him. Grim melancholy seeps like black ooze from the photograph. It bleeds out our television screens onto the floor of our living rooms, emitting the odor of decay. The distance between Gonzo and the shutterbug who snapped the photo suggests that even the companion joining him on this seaside stroll is hopelessly remote and removed. We are never so lonesome when amongst company, and Gonzo appears to have drifted off from a disconnected mate. Between two profound solitudes, the weirdo knows not where to turn, and has nowhere comforting to avert his gaze.

Perhaps Gonzo even came alone to stare into the ocean depths, and the photographer merely chanced upon this heart-rending scene of cosmic forlorn. That he is staring into the ocean is a remarkable statement and a masterstroke of the first or second rank. The ocean is not only symbolic of human origins, but is quite literally the source of our existence. It is the womb in which we gestated, and henceforth sprung from. The organism that crawled from the ocean to live on dry land could hardly have known what chain of events it put in motion. And we don't assume conscious motives for this singular amphibian. But surely there must be some plan behind all this? If we can assume the fertile churn of the oceans is mindless and without motive, then why not those same fertile churns of the universe? What drives life, and what aim does it have? All these questions arise in our minds when pondering the ocean, which for the ancients was even more mysterious than the larger universe is to us.

Jung suggested that mankind's awaking to himself involves first a "differentiation," from his environment.

Here is the ultimate portrayal of mankind's painful individuation from ecstatic, egoless identification with the All. That is truly the crisis Gonzo is facing, as are all of us moderns. There are said to be three stages in the healthy spiritual development of man. First, as infants and toddlers, we live in a state of unification with the world, and are unable to conceive ourselves as distinct or separate from what is physically external to us. As we grow, our minds begin to develop egos, a sense of self, distinction as a subject standing opposed, vis-à-vis, to what is external and objective. In short, standing face-to-face with the rest of the universe, from which we now feel cut off. The completion of this process—otherwise known as individuation—is the end of second stage, and the one we moderns and skeptics are most prone to becoming bogged down in.

Lastly, the mystical among us aim to achieve that oneness that was lost, albeit on a far more sophisticated level. As experienced adults, we can meld towards that same unification we once experienced as babes.

The imaginary borderline we've erected to separate ourselves from what is "world," if too firmly established, cuts us off from opportunity to experience the mystical joys of losing oneself in ecstatic communion with the All; of wholly submerging the ego and rejoining the universe in glorious Oneness. This third stage of human spiritual development might rightly be compared to the first, only now the experience of unification is colored and informed by a lifetime of learning, experience, and wisdom.

Because of this, it is also an experience infinitely more intense, and might be compared to achieving nirvana, spiritual revelation, or profound epiphany—as Christian mystics had it, it was like being filled up with the Lord and Creator's powerful grace. To live in an active state of communion with the universe is probably asking more from most people than they are capable of. But if there is a person capable of realizing this cognitive and spiritual condition, then maintaining it for prolonged periods of time, we call that person a true mystic and saint.

Where modern man is stuck—and has been now for several centuries—is the second stage. There are many who are simply incapable of that kind of true mystical experience, and the experience of mystics will always be exotic and foreign to them. Then there are others who actively fear mystical union with the All, as well they should—for it can be a fearful thing to encroach into the higher echelons of consciousness. And there is yet a third class. These are the people who are capable, and who possess the courage or tolerance for more extreme states of spiritual existence than the average fellow, but who remain weary of the mystical experience all the same. They consider it a danger because by definition it implies the abandonment of one's critical faculties and rational intellect.

While believing in the psychological reality of mystical states, prudent spiritualists don't unquestioningly believe mystics are attuned to external spiritual forces. Prudence itself argues that these mystics are only experiencing an altered state of mind. Many sober-minded souls fear deluding themselves so much that they try to avoid at all costs any kind of religious enthusiasm. They are scientifically inclined, and rationalistic. They are skeptical of losing themselves because the loss of self implies the loss of intellectual conscience. Intellectual conscience is the wakeful and observant eye in the back of our minds that never gives itself over completely. Not to an experience, an idea, or emotion.

This is done so that when we return to ourselves, our experience can be picked apart and analyzed. We question ourselves and cast doubt on our lucidity. In this sense, we are condemned to analytical thought, and can never truly enjoy an experience.

We know from history that predictions arrived at during mystical experiences are more often wrong than not. Certainly this is the case when the mystic speaks in specifics. An infamous example would be the famous Ghost Dance just prior to the Indian massacre at Wounded Knee. A Lakota shaman predicted the Great Spirit would soon recall the ancient ancestors back to life, and wipe the North American continent clean of white men. Soon thereafter, Indians would be restored as the superior culture from sea to sea. Things didn't quite work out that way, to say the least. Another example is the continued predictions about the end of the world. These dates come to pass uneventfully, with the world continuing to exist. And if a mystic speaks abstractly, there is no objective way to analyze their claims, but there is also no reason to take their claims seriously as anything other than observations on the kind or quality of an internal state of mind.

Mysticism is a tricky business. It may be impossible for these good souls the scientific rationalists to immerse themselves in Universal Oneness. Yet our very future may depend on them eventually being able to do so. An overenthusiastic and credulous religionist is capable of inflicting more damage than the most corrupt and opportunistic charlatan, but a weary mystic who keeps his intellectual conscience intact has the potential to lead us into a Golden Age.

If the wise and educated men of today are going to lead us headlong into our uncertain future, they may have to seek out more than common wisdom, and tap into the spiritual resources laying latent in every member of our species. A strong spiritual drive, tempered by the rational instinct, will yet give us the doorway out of the modern malaise. Is it possible that Gonzo, in this secretly profound characterization, represents the path modern man must take to regain his primitive intimacy with the universe and natural world? It would be wise to consider.

We know the source of Earthly life is the ocean. The origins of all living creatures can be traced back to the single and multi-celled organisms that arose in these salty waters. But the ocean as metaphor goes beyond that. That the ocean gave rise to life is mysterious, but that life began somehow in the first place is a greater mystery. To us the cosmos is our ocean. We stare into its vastness and wonder how inorganic material became living organisms. How does life arise materially out of non-living matter? Why does it do so? What internal or external forces compel lifeless matter towards that uncanny end? And from the basic components of organic life, how do we arrive materially at the conscious, self-reflective life of a human being? What is our purpose for existing, if purpose there be? Alienation from the World is not just a thing of today—we are literally hundreds of millions of years removed from our origin and birth as a species. What happened during that prehistoric time? Would it comfort us to know, or would it disturb us beyond all measure?

Equal in desolation to the portrait of Gonzo is the answer to the question "Where are we going?" There was a time when the answer to this question would have conjured up merry thoughts of a very optimistic kind. We are going to Heaven to be with God, the angels, and all our beloved who have passed away. Or we were going to go through another cycle of reincarnation on our long path towards enlightenment and escape from the cycle of birth and death. Or we are going to Elysian Fields to play in the tall grass with Pan and his nymphs.

True, there was always Hell and Hades and bad Karma. These never sounded nice. But they were the consequence of a life consumed by evil, and very few people actually believe themselves to be evil. Even those held a pretty rosy picture of their afterlife. And socially, a hundred and two hundred years ago mankind began to believe in true progress—political, technological, intellectual, and ethical. Even the most calculated realist couldn't help but become giddy at the new powers mankind wielded over Nature through his utilization of technology. Back when, it was "better living through chemistry," and visions of airy Utopia began once again to enter the dream-life of every man.

Today things appear to us quite differently. We now know with ever-sharpening clarity where we are going. It isn't pretty. Time carries us relentlessly downstream toward doom, death and annihilation. Dashed upon the rocks of our expiration date, non-existence shall be our eternal reward. We have detailed knowledge of what happens to our material body during the process of decomposition. For some people, the repulsive details alone are enough to inspire a kind of atheistic bent. How could this soulful being so full of love, fear, hope, hatred, and dreams come to such a disagreeable end? Why this consciousness embedded inextricably to meat and bone, food for worms and maggots? How much cleaner and less sickening to just ascend bodily into Heaven! Or at least evaporate into airy nothing. Our corporeality makes us wince with displeasure.

And does anybody really believe the fairy tale of personal immortality? Many profess too, even some of the most brilliant minds of our time. But is this belief really acceptable anymore? Was it ever? How would it even be possible? It remains a conviction begging for any shred of evidence. And though some insist there is at least no evidence *against* this wishful fantasy, I beg to differ. Senility, dementia, illness, and damage to the brain all demonstrate quite clearly that the state or condition of our mind is entirely contingent on the state and condition of the grey matter inside our skulls, the brain.

Brain and personality are interlinked—each one informs the other. The deterioration of the brain leads to a deterioration of the person. There may be some parsing philosophical arguments made in favor of personal immortality, but are these convincing to thoughtful, rational people? The simplest observation of life should demonstrate to us that mental states are contingent on physical condition. We watch the brain fall to pieces, and with it the person we once knew.

How is it we should assume that when the brain is completely dead and decomposing, there is somehow some release from the relationship? By what mechanism? When the brain dies, the mind dies, and when the mind dies, we die. To believe otherwise is infantile. This fact may make us uncomfortable. It may be disagreeable. But a disagreeable truth proves more useful than a beautiful lie. It's not that the fact of our annihilation at death must of necessity spur us to some kind of action, but it seems far more likely than the belief that we have an infinite amount of time at our disposal. Many critics of religion decry that such belief systems put the emphasis on life outside of life. That they make personal immortality a weightier matter than our lives right now, in this very instant.

Putting aside the matter of our personal fate, we must also acknowledge that our species is equally doomed to annihilation. Even if by some miracle we manage to survive for eons, one day our sun will die, and with it the Earth. This glowing orb that has benefited us for so long will become a red giant, expanding to engulf us in its hellish fires. Even if the sun's decreasing mass pushes our orbit farther out, saving us from engulfment, all water and atmosphere will be boiled off the planet. We're going to die here, assuredly. But how likely is it that humanity will continue to happily exist until those final breathtaking moments? What chance do we have, given our historical drive towards war, overpopulation, environmental degradation, and the entire slew of phenomena which seem to have predestined our destruction? Add to the list of manmade catastrophes asteroids, ice ages, viral pathogens, and so on, it's clear we stand on a precipice. End of Days anxieties have both secular and religious origins, and the utmost reasonableness tells us we are not long for this world.

As Kermit takes leave of Gonzo, he assures his beak-nosed buddy that he isn't alone, but rather, "distinct." After gazing at his picture, Gonzo corrects this friendly frog: "Distinct? More like extinct." Indeed, Gonzo, after meditating on his photographically captured isolation on the beach, says to himself, "Distinct? More like *extinct*." We human beings are merely the walking dead, doomed to die out and be forgotten in what may be one trillionth of a second considered in the span of cosmic time. Truly we are already extinct, in the sense that our fate is certain and sealed beyond any conceivable doubt.

***

Now left alone in the house, Gonzo prepares himself a breakfast of cold cereal. While it is not only the lonely and hurting who enjoy a milky bowl of cornflakes, the ease of the instant meal seethes with loneliness and alienation. Put together without fanfare or preparation, it is the quick and easy concoction for those who plan to dine alone. Families do of course enjoy instant rice, microwave meals and cereal—on occasion or regularly. For households burdened by lack of time or interest, these processed foods may even be the staple diet. But it is the sad, stoop-shouldered bachelor who first comes to mind when we think of the primary consumer of these flash-frozen, cellophane-covered meals in a cardboard box. We've seen them in the stores, and probably been ones ourselves. They stand in line before us at the supermarket. We peer into their baskets, and our heartstrings are pulled. We conduct our own transaction with the cashier in contemplative silence, and wonder about all the lonely people in the world.

The family dinner is such an icon of togetherness, that those of us without families of our own long for a communal mealtime, sharing stories and talking about our days. Presided over by Mom and Dad, this is no mere gabfest, but a special cementing of clan and familial bonds. It may sometimes feel like a chore to all get together for a meal, but what wonders when we do!

It is here at the nadir of his sorrow, from this moist and milky banquet of loneliness, that Gonzo receives the glimmer of hope that he's truly hungry for. It's a puzzling moment, yes, and Gonzo doesn't know any better than we do what to make of it. But Gonzo feels it. Somebody is reaching out to him through the fog, calling him home.

Gonzo pours himself a big bowl of Cap'N Alphabet cereal, a cross between Fruit Loops and Alpha-Bits. The letters magically rearrange to ask the question: R U THERE? And then, WATCH THE SKY.

That Gonzo should receive such communiqués through his alphabet cereal seems in some ways a senseless oddity. Are the filmmakers merely stretching for artificial eccentricity, or a thoughtless heaping-upon of zaniness? If so, to what end is all this quirkiness? Perhaps to dispel the gloomy, sickroom atmospherics so far coloring the film? To inject a neutralizing wackiness, therefore to remain at long last a *mere* Muppet movie? Surely there's a niblet of truth in this, as the mood within this world has already grown almost oppressively heavy, barely ten minutes in. A lifting burst of levity may be just the thing now to pull the viewer up from the dreary sludge, allowing for one revitalizing breath before plunging anew into the suffocating sadness of Gonzo's heartsick soul.

Yet before we stay the dogs of analysis, and dismiss the scene as giddiness for its own sake, let's ponder awhile. The adventurer in film theory always knows that what may seem like a throwaway line, continuity error, or other filmmaking "mistake," is very often the doorway to deeper readings. For starters, this is another nod to irrationalism.

This is once more a slight nod to the irrational and fantastic, to be sure. There is no medium by which the letters could have been arranged. This manipulation of the cereal bits is telekinetic. There is no radio or remote control that can manipulate wheat, flower, and sugar, and as far as we know no such medium could exist. All this may appear to be a sort of scholastic nit-picking, but there's good reason to focus so intently on this question. A scene where food acts as the conductor for the alien's message to Gonzo is repeated later in the film, only in the second sequence the food is a sandwich, and it is actually speaking. This element will be discussed in detail later, but it is my belief that the reason for this scene's fantastical elements is to suggest that Gonzo will have to push himself beyond the world of technical wizardry we inhabit in order to communicate with a more primitive element of himself, the irrational self.

Beyond this call to embrace irrationality, why must ask ourselves not why *cereal* was the chosen medium the aliens used to message Gonzo—but rather, why *alphabetic* cereal? Though we often take revolutionary historic advances for granted, we can hardly underestimate the effect adopting an alphabet had on human civilization and consciousness. Only, we should know here that the writers are invoking what is called the "alphabet theory," which has been developed by many legendary scholars. In short, these thinkers credit the development of an alphabet, and the abstract thinking it inspired, with the impetus toward science, law codes, an objective sense of history, monotheism, and even the notion of individualism itself.

If alphabet theory is even partially true, we must accept that the contemporary world, in all its beauty and terror, is partially built upon this edifice of letters. And since we now see what the end result of the rational society has led to, we can accept that the alphabet is in some ways the source of Gonzo's malaise, just as it is the source of both our malaise and our great hope.

R U THERE?

This is a pertinent question on so many levels. After all, mankind is the animal who asks: "Where do I come from? What am I? Where am I going?" So is Gonzo there? Is he really, truly there? Well, he is not. Not only is he not living in the moment, being there now, he is like a ghost hovering over reality, and is barely even a ghost.

Dumping his cereal out on the table, Gonzo discovers there is an eyeglass. Again, the association with the ocean is all too clearly made, as well as the fact that Gonzo is given a dated technology for his.

✶✶✶

In the next scene we are finally introduced to the exterior of COVNET, a sector of the military-industrial complex tasked with defending America and the Earth from extraterrestrial enemies. It is disguised as a cement factory (building the blocks of tomorrow), thereby "cementing" the connection between the military and major industry. Character actor Jeffrey Tambor plays K. Edgar Singer, a playful twist on the appellation of J. Edgar Hoover. Mister Tambor is the director of the Alien-Awareness Division at COVNET, which is charged with "identifying and neutralizing extraterrestrial threats." The existence of a clandestine military-industrial bureaucracy is part and parcel for the genre, and plants the film squarely within the world of sociologically concerned science fiction. No statement on modern humanity is complete without it. It is the very depiction of technological society run amok, allied with the forces of war and exploitation.

Tambor of course plays a paranoid bumbler. Why else do you cast Jeffrey Tambor, but to have a character who is paranoid and a bumbler? And though Tambor does indeed exhibit paranoiac tendencies, and is a bumbler to boot, his character is also vindicated. As the only one who takes seriously a string of recent alien communiqués, he is the only agent within his milieu willing to connect the dots. These dots turn out to be Gonzo's extraterrestrial relations trying to make contact with him. He is an agent whose paranoia makes him effective at his job, and it is shown that, despite his reaction to the truth, he is at least able to see the reality of the crisis before him. Unlike his superiors, he can recognize a threat when he sees one.

Tambor's character teaches us that, "just because you're paranoid does not mean they're not after you." For his commitment to the pursuit of truth, however misguided, he is portrayed somewhat heroically. Yet he is also the film's villain, and so presents us with a serious thematic complexity, as we shall see.

Casting in film is an art form unto itself, and assigning a Jew to the role of K. Edgar Singer was a stroke of inspiration. Singer is a rather common Jewish surname. Why is it necessary that the character K. Edgar Singer be Jewish? The symbolic resonance of the name is startling. Singing, though today considered mostly as an entertainment, has a unique place in mankind's evolutionary history. Singing predates language, and certainly played an integral role in the social life of our pre-human ancestors, just as it still does in birds. Of particular interest is the "calls" of various humanoid-like apes such as the chimpanzee. Though we must broaden our definition of song to include these calls, most primatologists accept them as a primitive form of song.

The voice was the first musical instrument, and primitives considered singing so awesome an act that in many creation myths a people or tribe is said to have been sung into existence by some god or other. Singing continues to be an essential function in all religious activities, but especially among more primitive cultures. Among these cultures it is still used to relate the people's history, celebrate rites of passage, and invoke the gods. If we accept that these are the primordial functions of singing, then we must of necessity accept my interpretation of the symbolic value of Jeffrey Tambor's K. Edgar Singer.

To begin, there is serious speculation within the world of physical anthropology that pre-human singing itself led to the development of language through the evolution of a lowered larynx. This would mean that singing was the fundamental catalyst for the slow rise of human consciousness, as there could hardly be consciousness as we understand it without there first being the existence of language. Language, at least in a rudimentary form, is thought to preexist consciousness. That repeated grunts and growls could be used to signify certain things, and later certain concepts, would lead to our entire system of linguistic symbolism.

In the metaphorical, poetic, and traditionally Catholic approach to that most famous of Judeo-Christian texts, *Genesis* and its Creation Story, it is thought eating of the Forbidden Fruit on The Tree of Knowledge is an allegory for the development of consciousness. By achieving consciousness—as Genesis would have it, attaining to the knowledge reserved for God—we became self-aware, and conscious of the difference between good and evil. Prior to eating the fruit, Adam and Eve (as mythical stand-ins for Man and Woman), lived in the Garden of Eden, a Paradise where there was no worry and no ethical dilemmas, because there was no self-awareness.

The state of mind described in this creation narrative is an analog to our pre-human lack of self-reflexive consciousness. Before the rise of such a consciousness, which would have deprived us of any but the most rudimentary awareness of ourselves as individual beings (thus saving us from existential anxiety), or any but the most primordial sense of right and wrong actions (thus saving us from the sting of conscience or any true reflection on ethics). In social primates, what is "wrong" is what gets one upbraided by a hierarchically superior member of the group, just as it would have been with our own primate ancestors. There is no "guilty conscience" per se.

So the very Fall of Man was unquestionably a consequence of attaining consciousness, which was itself an indirect result of our ability to sing. We shall then be speaking accurately if we say there was a "Singer" present during the greatest event in the history of mankind, and arguably in the history of organic life on this planet. We don't fool ourselves into thinking that there was a sudden moment we attained consciousness, but instead recognize it as a gradual process that took eons, and is still an ongoing concern. However, would it not then be appropriate, even necessary, that there also be a "Singer" present during humanity's next great advance in consciousness?

This theme has some precedence in the genre of serious speculative fiction. To consider but one well-known example, Kubrick's masterpiece, *2001: A Space Odyssey*. The film depicts two major stages or shifts in human consciousness, and singing is present at both, just as the mysterious black monolith is. Both elements serve to mark the death-knell of an older cognitive state, while simultaneously "singing into existence" another very different, vastly more complex one.

During the first shift, from simian to technologically advanced human, the singing is the ferociously triumphant screams of an anthropoid ape as the basic concept of technology dawns on him. Famously, his screams are the vocals accompanying the easily recognizable first moment to Richard Strauss's "Also Sprach Zarathustra," a score inspired by yet another famous work dealing with radical leaps in human consciousness, Nietzsche's *Thus Spoke Zarathustra* (a book in which singing is considered essential to enlightenment).

The next leap in consciousness, from technologically advanced human to the ambiguously conceived "star-child," is marked by the disturbingly human-like singing of HAL, who in one of the most famous sequences in film graces astronaut Dave Bowman with an eerie version of the popular tin-pan alley tune "Daisy Bell."

All this is to imply that K. Edgar Singer is to be the "singer" presiding over a revolution in human consciousness. I hesitate to belabor the point about Judaic elements in *Muppets From Space*, but because I consider this essay to be a comprehensive and *exhaustive* treatment of the film, I must risk tedium for the sake of good scholarship.

Apology made, the character of K. Edgar Singer could only have been Jewish. As we said, the primitive uses of singing were to relate history, invoke the gods, and celebrate rites of passage. By being a Jew, this particular Singer provokes associations with the Judeo-Christian history that are woven inextricably into the fabric of Western Civilization. This, by the way, includes the development of Modern Science, which today we falsely imagine was opposed to institutionalized religion. In fact the two were closely linked until the rise of an educated, financially powerful commercial class during the 1700's. It is not within the scope of this essay, but suffice to say this is a commonly understood precept in the history of science.

Because Singer is also associated through his position at COVNET with the most advanced technology of industrial civilization, the shadow of his symbolic umbrella covers our historical progress from early apes to those of us living today. As for invoking gods, we see that our traditional Judeo-Christian God has been invoked by none other than Gonzo (who is also Singer's doppelganger, as we shall learn), and that it appeared this old God was not to be invoked, nor even properly evocable. And as concerns singing during important rites-of-passage, we have already covered that thoroughly and altogether brilliantly in the previous passages.

That Singer's middle initial is K. lends another clue as to the proper conceptualization of him as a character. To those of us of a literary bent, the figure of K. will hardly require discussion. But for the benefit of the unlearned, I shall now generously provide an introduction. Josef K. in *The Trial*, and simply K. in *The Castle*, was the fictional alter-ego of yet another great Jewish writer grappling with the existential crisis the modern world had hoisted upon humanity's shoulders, Franz Kafka.

Granted, Kafka had more to fret about than most of us. Ever in poor health, the Czech writer was oppressed by his overbearing father, stuck in an unfulfilling office job as an insurance officer, and a Jew under the shadow of the Nazi buildup prior to World War II and the Holocaust. Two of Kafka's brothers died as children, and two of his sisters died in concentration camps. His two most famous novels combine the absurd, surreal, and mundane as the hero in both books attempts to navigate his way through strange, shadowy, and sinister bureaucracies.

Though interpretations of Kafka's work are as varied as the men and women who study his works, most scholars, including his literary executor Max Brod, agree that his absurdist tales are religious allegories, and describe mankind's apparently futile, disastrous, and picaresque attempts at salvation or communion with the Sacred. Like Gonzo, K. and Josef K. seek an entrance or doorway out of the absurd world into the radiant glory of redemption.

It is instructive that in Kafka's novella *The Metamorphosis*, singing is associated with a radical shift in consciousness in the protagonist Gregor Samsa. only his shift leads him into a final renunciation of his humanity, due mostly to his reverse-apotheosis into a giant insect. In the final scenes, Gregor is lured out of the room where he has been kept by the beautiful violin-playing of his sister. The violin is the instrument which comes closest to mimicking the tonality of the human voice. For leaving his room and disturbing the guests at his sister's recital, his father throws an apple at him in order to chase him off, and the apple becomes lodged in his back.

The wound eventually leads to the infection that causes his death. The apple of course representing the "Forbidden

Fruit" in the Garden of Eden, which imparted the knowledge of God unto those who tasted of it. In *The Metamorphosis*, the apple also pushes the protagonist toward a forbidden knowledge. But rather than a shift "upward," the awareness leads Gregor "downward," into a recognition of his own essential meaninglessness.

Here it will also be necessary to say a few words on COVNET. COVNET is a thinly disguised phonetic rendering of the word COVENANT. The most famous covenant in Western History is, of course, the Covenant Yahweh—or as we know Him today, God—made with the Jewish people. Particularly those made with the patriarchs Abraham and Moses. The Covenant was that Yahweh (God) would protect the Jews, and bestow upon them spiritual and material blessings, and make of them a great nation, so long as they submitted to Yahweh's will and obeyed His commandments. That Judaism has conquered half the world through Christianity is evidence that perhaps the Covenant was fulfilled, although in the a twist of fate so out-of-the-blue only Yahweh Himself, through the exercise of His omniscience, could have possibly seen it coming.

The so-called New Covenant is that Jesus, as the sacrificed Son of Yahweh, is the doorway through which salvation is to be achieved. Basically, the new message was follow the commandments, but also love your neighbor and don't entertain doubts about the truth of Christianity or the factual existence of Yahweh, lest you be severely punished. Unlike traditional Judaism, the gifts to be earned were eternal life and blessedness, not more goats and kids.

As *Space Muppets* suggests, both the old covenant and the newer one have lost their currency, and whether it is due to Yahweh not holding up his end of the bargain or mankind, a new way is sought, one where the concept of a covenant will not even be considered, unless it is considered derisively as an atavistic religious doctrine more appropriate to tribal peoples than to mankind in his contemporary context.

There is another covenant in Western History, just as dramatic and probably far more important to those of us living today, and that is the implied covenant between Science, along with it's handmaid Technology, and we human beings here on Planet Earth, you and I and everybody else. Our covenant with Science is that we allow it to go poking and prodding into the mysteries of existence, but only so long as it continues to provide us with the benefits we crave. Science can peak and peer and probe into forbidden things, so long as the scientific endeavor provides recognizable benefits.

In short, why do we allow the risk of developing a super-virus capable of wiping out civilization, or chemical advances that pollute the environment, or weapons technology that threatens us all? Because we may get a cure for polio, a vaccine for AIDS, a new system of flight or terrestrial conveyance, or a real discovery of the Fountain of Youth, based on a scientific approach to the problem of immortality and aging. We tell science, "Look, we'll put up with your destruction and dismantling of everything we cherish and hold dear, but you better fucking wow us with some of that magical-realist scientific shit."

Prior to World War I, especially, but even up until the commencement of World War II, Science and Technology were expected to create a Paradise for human beings on Earth, and usher us into a new Golden Age of nothing but happiness, general enlightenment, rational social organization, and unprecedented political freedom. But what both world wars taught us is that science and technology is put to destructive, even evil uses in equal proportion to good ones, and it is hardly even clear anymore whether many of the "good" uses can still be considered utterly beneficent. For example, the development of psychotropic drugs, various genetically engineered seeds, and toxic chemicals such as flame retardants.

Further, it seems unlikely that a purely "rational" existence would be fulfilling to the spirit of humankind, and might actually represent the high-water mark of dehumanization. Thus we see that the Covenants of both Science and Religion have proved themselves bunkum. If not completely so, in many of their essentials.

Singer conceives of the universe as inherently threatening. As pointed out, this is thematically sound. The "singer" being associated with shifts to a higher state of consciousness, and the birth of new worlds, it would be jarring if Singer were to view the burgeoning modern paradigm as anything less than hostile. Transitions to higher states of consciousness of necessity cause anxiety. It is a New Age foolishness that would convince us these transformations are gracefully smooth, and without agony. Birth always comes with some pain. The individual who is ahead of his or her time is prone to self-doubt, second-guessing, and crippling bouts of alienation and anomie. These members of the *avant garde* are motherless babes, suckling on the rotted teats of a corpse. In retrospect, they are seen as heroic. Yet their utility is almost never recognized during their living years, and their isolation is ever a source of suffering.

Though we are encouraged to see Singer as reactionary and a bit asinine, he is actually the character most in touch with reality. Firstly, of course, though the film shows his concerns about a hostile alien race as being mistaken, there's no reason we should assume if an alien race is intent on visiting us, that they will do so with the friendliest of intentions. When we step up to a higher level of analysis, Singer is seen as the only character aside from Gonzo who views the Death of God as an existential threat.

Singer is reminiscent of a character from one of Nietzsche's most famous aphorisms, *The Parable of the Madman*. Though this anonymous man of madness only appears in a few brief paragraphs, among those in the know In this brief parable, a man runs into a town square, proclaiming the Death of God. It being just His manner is so frantic that the atheists who hear him mock his dramatic response. These thinkers who have done away with God do not yet understand the consequences of their actions. Singer is the madman who understands what is truly at stake. Because in the face of the modern calamity he cannot keep his cool, he is set up as a clown.

Singer's assistant, his right-hand man, is the likable and infinitely amiable Bobo the Bear. Bobo is a comical rendering of Boris the Bear, the unofficial mascot of Soviet Russia. The friendly Bobo represents a tamed and amicable Soviet Union. Though astute analysts still consider Russia an antagonist to the United States, there is still a lingering afterglow of optimism about the possibilities for world peace in a post-Cold War Era. Even to this day, but it was especially true in 1999, before the September Eleventh attacks and the wars that followed. For the makers of Muppets from Space, who had lived their entire lives in the shadow of the Cold War, it must have been very appealing to no longer have to fear the Soviets.

Bobo isn't neutered, he is reasonable and rational, and stands in contrast to the intensely paranoid shenanigans of Singer. There is certainly some insinuation on the part of the writers that the overly dramatized fear of the Soviets was always a bit of political theater. Politicians used the concept of the Evil Empire to further their own agendas. And while this may have been true, we must remember that this film is operating on many levels, and that the political is only the surface and most shallow of these levels. Singer's real fear is modern melancholy and nihilism, and what seems like his desperate desire for an enemy in fact represents two drives.

First, he recognizes that there is a true enemy out there, and he has projected the encroaching nihilism onto the alien beings, and does not see one apart from the other. Secondly, his instincts drive him to have an enemy, which we may scoff at, but quite possibly to our detriment. For having an enemy has many uses, and an archenemy can in fact be a spur to life.

Regardless of the excesses of Cold War rhetoric, we must also remember that having the Soviets as our enemy spurred us to some remarkable achievements. Achievements that linger in our imagination as among our proudest moments as a nation. The Soviet launch of Sputnik drove us to compete in the Space Race, and to eventually surpass the Soviets by putting a man on the moon, an achievement that would have our ancestors' heads spinning. It didn't take long after the dissolution of the USSR for American politicians to go searching for another enemy to fill the void. The events of September Eleventh provided us such an enemy in radical Islam. But because this enemy is much more ambiguous, it's much easier to see through as rhetoric. Moreover, use of Radical Islam as an enemy does not necessarily spur us to as readily recognizable achievements as did our rivalry with the Soviets, who at least were a nation. The lack of a worthy rival deprives us of a scale by which we can measure our own progress.

For several generations the Other was a well-defined Soviet Union. We are now in need of a new enemy. Having an enemy who represents the antithesis to one's own core values is a great way to solidify one's personal identity, and also tends to put less pressing existential matters on the backburner of concern. "One must first have bread to feel that cosmic dread," as the poets say. The Islamic Fundamentalists may serve as a convincing enemy for a while, but I would surmise their retrograde impulses will not appeal for long even in their own regions of the globe. Still, as an enemy they will save us for a while from the discomforting conclusions that must be drawn from contemplation of the vacuous and dreaded universe.

In this case, Fukayama's famous End of History—meaning the end of massive political struggle here on Earth—could lead to an existential and spiritual crisis which humanity may be incapable of bearing. And in particular, if there ever comes a day when world peace is achieved, and all our international tensions resolved, we will as a collective species have to turn our sights on the cosmos itself as our dreaded foe.

It may be here where the makers of *Muppets From Space* steered their course foolishly. It pains me to entertain the possibility in a film so tightly conceived, and for that reason I have decided to lend them the benefit of the doubt. I will for now stick to my belief that the casting of Jeffrey Tambor, and the depiction of K. Edgar Singer as an utterly buffoonish character, was not a careless misstep, but a creative decision the inspiration for which issued forth from the among the very highest planes of intellectual art.

True, the necessity of him representing Judeo-Christian history, and of mankind's often bumbling attempts at higher states of consciousness, lends itself to just the kind of satirical buffoonery of a Jeffrey Tambor. And as a lampoon on J. Edgar Hoover there may also be some justification. Though I did not know the man, and therefore whether or not he was deserved of lampooning, I have read his rare manifesto on Communism, and found the critical thinking skills on display to be more than a little piddling.

As scholarship or philosophy it was nothing to learn from. However, as propaganda it may have been a work of sheer brilliance, and propaganda must be assessed according to different standards than art or scholarship. In addition, I'm not quite certain I buy into the political left's caricature of Hoover, which may simply be the vengeance of spoiled poofballs in the entertainment and culture industries.

A paranoid state of mind like Singer's may be necessary to the thorough thinking-out of strategic defense plans. One really needs to be a Hippie from La-La Land to believe the need for national security is all an illusion fed by the fantasies of irrationally frightened men. There are real threats in the real world to our sovereignty and stability—and in a nation-state security is essential to political freedom—and it takes a certain kind of imagination to roam through the smorgasbord of dark possibilities. Didn't everybody say that the real cause of September 11th was a failure of imagination? That because nobody considered it possible, it thereby became a possibility? Of course this was a cover-up, because obviously it had been considered as a possibility, and the president was even warned about it a month in advance. Still, I'm sure that generally speaking it held true. The people in the FBI and CIA and NSA had become careerist bureaucrats, and not men like Singer, who obviously put the job above their careers.

Men like Singer are necessary to our safety, and men like General Luft, his military supervisor, are a danger in the presence of a real threat because they are too skeptical and, being aged, tend to be far more conservative. But if General Luft represents willful blindness or the rational skepticism of bureaucracies, and Singer overreaching paranoia, what are we to surmise? But after all, Singer is vindicated because he is in fact correct about the alien visitation, though incorrect about their hostility to humans. We must then conclude Singer has an eye for the facts, but his interpretations are off.

Therefore, to follow our theme, Singer must see that the godlessness and meaningless of the vast cosmos does indeed pose a threat, but is still blind to the possibility it may also pose an opportunity for new kinds of joy. This leads Singer to be a sympathetic character, at least partially. That General Luft always denies Singer the validation he seeks emphasizes to us in the audience that the threat to humankind is not to be thought of as a military matter, but a matter of each man's individual relationship to the potentially malevolent cosmos, Gonzo and Singer merely representing two styles of approach. The former's resigned and saddened, the latter's aggressive and panicked.

***

Band guy asks Gonzo if he wants his latest issue of Insanity Fair, and Gonzo says, I'll get it later. Kermit asks what Gonzo is doing on the roof, Rizzo says his breakfast cereal told him to sit on the roof. Talk about whole grain and nuts. Gonzo will enter into irrationality.

Meanwhile Gonzo, in response to written messages he has received through his alphabetic cereal, has climbed onto the roof of his home in an attempt to make contact with what he suspects are his relatives. The spyglass he holds in his hands acts as a lightning rod, and Gonzo is struck by a lightning bolt. This bursting bolt of electricity fantastically transports him to distant sectors of the cosmos. Whether he is transported to the nether realms of the universe or of his own mind is an open question, but in either case the possibilities for interpretation are rich.

The lightning bolt itself echoes with unbound symbolic resonance. A thunderbolt was the weapon Zeus hurled at enemies whom he felt were acting impiously. This was later carried over into popular Christian usage, wherein God may strike somebody down in anger over an impiety or blasphemy. In Judeo-Christian theology, the greatest sin is to fall out of trust with God, to lose faith in Him.

Despite what awful calamities befall you, always trust that God has allowed these scourges because they somehow serve our best interest. From our finite perspective we may not understand, but by accepting that God understands, we can come to terms with our sufferings. Gonzo, then, is the ultimate blasphemer, the exact opposite of the Biblical Job. By foregoing his Bar Mitzvah in the earlier scenes, he has in effect denied the providence and wisdom of God, and seeks consolation elsewhere. He must therefore be stricken with the avenging thunderbolt, which is what we call chastisement to the tune of up to a billion volts.

That Gonzo has not only received the punishing bolt, but was in some sense petitioning it, means that he has accepted the guilt of abandoning God. He knows what direction his path must follow, even at the risk of damnation. To inherit his destiny he must break from the father in a quest that is both heroic and demonic. As we saw in the parable of the madman, the atheists assembled in the square hadn't taken upon their shoulders the massive responsibility for killing God. Their wont was to ignore the consequences. Today, before we are able to posit a new agnostic and secular spirituality, we must first concede that denying the old gods loads us down with a burdened conscience. We must first feel the pangs of guilt for denying God, and from that point venture forth on our spiritual quest.

Significantly, this is the first time the film takes a turn towards true positivity. It suggests that if Gonzo can only perceive his despair as an opportunity for advancement, rather than an intractable morass, he will find a newfound zest for life. It may be that his descent to the bottom has left him with nothing more to do but rise, rise into the heights—free and fancy, soaring where eagles dare. At first Gonzo is frightened by being catapulted through the cosmic void. But when he finally pulls himself together, the exhilaration of flight overcomes him. He dives and soars like an acrobatic skydiver, intoxicated with the rush of this new lightness to his being.

Gonzo's ecstasy is such that even as he approaches a pink nebular cloud, eagerly exclaims "I bet this is going to be painful!!!" Gonzo is in fact excited by the prospect of experiencing physical pain. The agony will wash him clean. Human beings know at some visceral level that physical suffering can be redemptive. Not only does motif play out in our myths and archetypes, we know it to be true from personal experience. Sensual pain awakens us like nothing else, reminding us that we are, in fact, alive. We are blood and tissue, have volume and mass, are sensate and vulnerable. Pain snaps us out of the cloudy haze, and can bring us to strict focus and attention.

The great majority of us sleepwalk through the day, settled into a general rut that gives us stability, but at the cost of constant numbness. As the days stack up, we risk extinguishing our human spirit completely. We yearn for an experience that will make us feel truly alive. As foolhardy young things, we actively sought these experiences out, hungry for the thrill of adventure. As we age, these ecstasies become less frequent, if they occur at all. If we should chance to feel them, the heights they lift us to are far below the ones we experienced when young.

Gonzo barrels through the pink cloud, and confirms his own suspicions, laughing as if the brutal scrapes were really tickling. "It does, it does," he laughs—it *does* hurt. But it hurts so very *good*.

Aside from the emotional benefits of pain, we must remember that there can be no birth without pain. And let there be no doubt that in this scene, Gonzo is being born anew. The space-cloud Gonzo courses through is pink. It clearly represents the Feminine in general, and the birth canal in particular. We are literally watching Gonzo being born again. That his flight is involuntary is but one more indication this is a birth, as all of us are given life against our wishes.

If we very carefully watch the scene in which Gonzo is struck by lightning, and pause the film just as this bolt strikes his body, we'll notice that it hits him directly in the lower abdomen. The belly button, where, if he were human, would be the plug of his umbilical cord. So Gonzo's break from God, his insolence, is connected thematically to his rebirth. He has rejected the sterile element of the father in favor of the birthing element of the mother. Likewise, though we may despair at the decay of traditional society, might also begin to sense the wondrous possibilities for renewal that are presented by this decay. A break from ancient modes of thought is a blank canvas upon which we can paint new pictures and write our own stories. The old absolutely has to die for the new to be born, as ever.

After tunneling through the Cosmic Womb, or Space Vagina, Gonzo is approached by two Cosmic Fish. These fish are apparently related to Hindu mystics and their brand of cosmic consciousness, for they speak with Indian accents. It is hardly my place to lecture on Hinduism and how its tenets are represented in this film. The religion is as alien to me as Gonzo's brethren. I will say, however, that the Cosmic Fish offer Gonzo tea (and speak English) forces us to assume these ostensibly "traditionally Indian" Cosmic Fish represent post-colonial Indians, and not those maintaining the swami and yogi meditative traditions of eras long past.

What this tells us is that the spiritual renewal Gonzo seeks will not be found in Eastern religion. So often starry-eyed Westerners bury their heads in systems of Eastern thought, under the presumption that they will find enlightenment precisely there. But this is the common response of those who are running from modernity, and not embracing it as the foundation upon which a new spirituality will be built. It may be necessary that Western and Eastern thought be wed together in our souls, but that is only a precursor to what must of necessity be new.

No less than Western religion, Eastern religion arose among civilizations radically different from our own. While they may have offerings worthy of inclusion in the spirituality of the future, they can do nothing more than assist us toward the breaking dawn. And besides, modern India is moving full-bore into modernity, having adopted our social institutions to a much greater degree than we have theirs. As this daunting technological civilization uproots them further and further from the earth, they will find themselves saddled with the same spiritual needs as us. We are that much further beyond them, and are two steps deeper into the future. There could well come a time when global culture is so homogenous—even speaking a single universal language—that all nations will be at the same point, but that time has not quite come.

It remains to be explained why Gonzo's cosmic encounter is with fish and not, for instance, a wise old owl. It's not immediately obvious that a pair of trout belong loitering in deep space more than any other creature. Yet there is something about this scene that we accept, and probably has to do with the connection we make between space and the ocean itself. Though to some degree we've mapped and conquered the ocean, for eons the great bodies of water were for our kind the "Final Frontier."

More relevant than our association of space with the ocean, however, is the rich symbolic history of the fish. A quick Google search or survey of academic journals will bear this out quite nicely, so I will only touch briefly on the topic. In short, the fish is a stand-in image for the vagina. As we live in a world fairly devoid of rich symbolism, and in which ancient symbolism has had the meaning transferred, we can only really speculate as to how this association came about. But at the risk of being vulgar, it is still common today to associate the vagina's taste and odor with just the slightest bit of fishiness. A clean vagina has a very pleasant odor, yet may still remind the sniffer a bit of the old ichthys. And this of course is in modern times, when our level of hygiene is orders of magnitude above the ancients. Therefore, vaginas throughout history would have tended to smell far fishier than they do today.

What is also apparent is that this association of odors was probably rather pleasant to these ancestors. Fish and the bounty of the ocean would be wonderful to associate with the vagina, and would have created an immediate connection to the ocean as the source of Life itself. It is only in our clean and clinical world of refrigeration and grocery stores that we can come to associate fish with decay and rot.

It is that ancient pagans in particular associated the fish with reproduction, and the word for fish may be etymologically rooted in the Babylonian word for "womb." In ancient Greek, the word "delphos" is used for both fish and womb. The fish also has a more general association with female genitals, as indicated by the Goddess of Ephesus, often depicted wearing a fish over her vagina like a scaly merkin. In sub-continental Asia the fish also has associations with reincarnation, and thus rebirth. One Indian religious group thought that fish housed the souls of the deceased, and that to eat one of these fish during a certain fertility ritual was to release the soul for reincarnation as a newborn child.

In any case, clearly Gonzo has encountered the vagina at the far end of the birth canal. Thus he is metaphorically right at the entryway to his new state of existence. Gonzo is treading water, clearly suggesting a final swim in amniotic fluid. What further solidifies the association, however, is what the two fish instruct him to do. They encourage him to mow the lawn, and "trim it well." Among the things that most go trimmed these days, we tend to think of the pubic hair rather than the lawn.

Because the Fish represents the procreative energies of the female, it seems as if Gonzo must summon his latent Feminine energies if he is to succeed in achieving his spiritual awakening. Historically we could take this hint to mean that Gonzo must summon the spiritual powers of irrationalism and the emotional, which a male artist may summon before undertaking a serious creative project. Using his masculine will to shape and mold, he will try to sculpt these energies into something magnificent.

In this cosmic womb is where Gonzo finds the Cosmic Fish, who, having cosmic knowledge of secret things, inform him that his people are looking for him. After telling him to mow a message in his lawn, one visible from space which will notify his kin of his whereabouts on Earth, the Fish send him off with a "May the Fish be with you." This scene has many implications. Gonzo is for the first time informed he is not alone in the universe. This association of the Fish with the Force from the *Star Wars* series implies that some Force or other is necessary for Gonzo to harness during his rebirth.

Regarding the potency of the irrational, there is a divide amongst academic feminists. Many feminist thinkers believe associating women with irrationalism and uncontrolled emotion is to think derogatorily about them. Other philosophers, such as Nietzsche, emphasized the irrational feminine spirit as the major propellant force in every person's life, and that our rational, masculine intellect merely steers the course, aiming and adjusting while we surf the wave of feminine potency. The irrational drive then is both destructive and creative—the mania of a berserker and the mania of an artist. Its drive is to tear down old systems of thought, yes, but merely for the provision of another blank canvas, another opportunity to discharge new stores of energy and release orgasmic creative tensions which have been storing up to explode.

Because rationality is a late development in organic mental life, and irrationality closer to the true and deepest character of life, rational drive will never provide Gonzo with a satisfactory conclusion to his cosmic quandary. The rational intellect will be necessary to give it shape, but it itself does not command the kind of powerful spiritual energies required. Indeed, though the aliens themselves are in fact real, and Gonzo himself is an alien, the experience with the Cosmic Fish may only have played out in Gonzo's electrocuted mind.

Of course, the Cosmic Fish may have only been mental projections verbalizing what Gonzo was subconsciously already certain of. This interpretation may even be more fruitful analytically than the one which posits Gonzo as having actually traveled through space and actually contacted

Cosmic Fish. For in that case we could explore numerous new possibilities, such as the possibility the entire episode is happening only in Gonzo's mind, leaving the climax of the film to serve as a meditation on the nature of mass hallucinations, delusion, and groupthink.

At the end of this Gonzo interrupts the card game, a game of randomness and chance, but also of ordered chaos. By touching Rizzo he infects him with lightning, and his four aces are burnt to a crisp (?) He grabs the keys to the lawn mower and mows the message I AM HERE. James Brown Get Up Offa That Thing, runs over a cat, a pussy. He is trimming the lawn, exposing his female genitalia.

Uses of the Dionysian. Nietzsche is misunderstood. His ecstasy is a sober one, not a party, not an orgy, not a libertine or partying mode. The idea is to use the Dionysian. The party.

When he is struck, he tells Rizzo and Pepe the Prawn that his relatives are telling him what to do and he does, so they get him to build a Jacuzzi. Then some people steal his cake. All this is one more suggestion that the existence of friends really doesn't address the primary concern here.

Band guy asks Gonzo if he wants his latest issue of Insanity Fair, and Gonzo says, I'll get it later.

***

That Gonzo has accepted irrationality as a means to truth is lent credence in the scenes following his encounter with the

Cosmic Fish. Gonzo begins to display what are considered classic signs of madness and paranoid delusion. He wears a tinfoil hat, he maniacally mows the lawn in the late night. He runs a cat over with his rider mower, and seems not much to care. Kermit watches him somberly from the window, not sure what to make of Gonzo's behavior.

Everybody thinks he has completely lost his marbles. All who know him think him mad. Wishing to indulge his fantasies, the two basement scientists Beaker and Bunsen Honeydew outfit Gonzo with a helmet that receives radio waves. This is futile, because we know that the aliens do not transmit this way. This method's failure is once again to demonstrate that Gonzo must put himself outside of the technological context in which he swims to make true contact with himself. However, as a device to move the plot forward, this move is ingenious.

At the very moment his hat is being tested, the rest of the Muppets are upstairs watching Miss Piggy's television debut. Miss Piggy is representative of the Feminine. She is all things a woman is: vain, ambitious, clever, and, when need be, nurturing. Men fall in love with her and lose themselves, and Kermit always needs her to feel whole.

Miss Piggy is in a pickle. She is the Feminine in a Masculine world. Civilization-building has historically been a man's work, and for that reason modern society is said by critics to be built disproportionately upon testosterone. It's impossible to say whether or not civilization would have involved in a significantly different way had women been given more influence on political and economic concerns. Regardless, the

Feminine now asserts itself wherever and whenever it can. Women are given forums for influencing law and society, and continue to take an ever greater role in leading the nation. While men still hold most of the positions of power, the ladies are gaining ground. This may help restore a kind of balance to the world, and any emergence of the Feminine should be seen as a step forward, so long as it does not aim to emasculate the Masculine.

That the Feminine assertion is demonstrated by Miss Piggy. A career woman, she is cunning in her quick climb to the top. She has begun the day as a "gofer" on the set of a news program, but has ambitions to become an anchor. She has in fact misrepresented her role at the television station to her friends. This leaves her with an intense desire to save face, but it may also be seen as envisioning the end goal. It is instructive that Miss Piggy wants to be in mass media as well. Her message of the Feminine drive to be heard must be communicated to the masses.

The intro to the program, UFO Mania, depicts Shelley Snipes as anchorwoman, calling upon anyone who has recently been contacted by aliens to come down to the studio. Gonzo, taking this as a communication from his brethren that he should meet them at the studio, rushes away on his lawn mower to the station. Meanwhile, it turns out that Shelley Snipes is stuck at the airport, and the show is just about to air. The producer, Rob Schneider at his brilliant best, tells himself that he will not panic, but in the next moment does.

The male is in crisis as to his role these days. He realizes that he must rely on the feminine, as Piggy winks her way onto the news desk of UFO Mania. The show opens with her unskillfully bumbling her way through the lines of cue cards. This to indicate that the new uses of the feminine will not be constrained by scripts, rote concepts, or expected roles. There is a new narrative in town.

As the show fumbles, Gonzo jumps out in front of the cameras to announce that he was contacted by his breakfast cereal just that morning, and that the Cosmic Fish confirmed to him that his alien kin were trying to contact him. Gonzo exposes himself to the world, says "I am here." At first it seems like a disaster, and it prompts Kermit and the gang, viewing the shenanigans from their living room, to head down to the station to rescue Gonzo. A situation they had been trying to ignore has now become critical, and they must act on it.

Singer is of course tuned into UFO Mania back at COVNET, and sees Gonzo mentioning he'd been contacted by aliens. He sends two henchman to kidnap him.

They arrive at the studio and by declaring themselves representatives from the alien protection services, trick Gonzo into entering the limo for a ride back to COVNET. As they leave through the back door, Rizzo the Rat in tow, Miss Piggy accosts the group, saying she needs Gonzo for her exclusive interview. She realizes very quickly that these men are not who they say they are.

What ensues is not a representation of the battle of the sexes per se, but rather, a battle of the genders. There is a rather frank sexual dimension to the fight between Miss Piggy and this dark-suited agent of COVNET. They both spring into fighting stances, mentioning their credentials as warriors. His are typically masculine, hers feminine. They punch and fight and are almost orgiastic with the blows. The agent at last seems to take her down and wrestles her into a headlock, forcing her mouth towards his genitals in the ultimate demonstration of submission. It is here that Piggy slams the man's vulnerable testicles, and crushes them in her hands. The emasculation of the masculine is complete.

Afterward we see what is almost a scene of post-coital interrogation. There is a plate of cheese, grapes, and wine set out, the glasses half empty or more. The Agent is tied up in bondage, and Piggy pulls information from him. It's clear that torture wasn't used, but rather the cunning arts of seduction. After this breakdown, Piggy dumps the agent into the well, which clearly represents an attempt to push him back inside the vagina, to infantilize him.

There is much to think about here. Women have always been a mystery to men, and there is no literature of any age which does not bear this out. Today, as women become more powerful, and are loosed from their bondage, we think we begin to understand them because their most vocal advocates seem to be telling us what women want. These are of course women in the media, who claim the banner of feminist and propose to speak for all women. One sees them at their most miffed when a successful woman distances herself from Feminism and feminists.

However, if I may speak anecdotally, in my time I have know many women, romantically and otherwise, who were slightly repulsed by the attitudes of feminists, and turned off by their air of militancy and the chip that was somehow placed on their shoulders. All these women, might I had, were educated and independent and professional.

I would caution the young man of today, and at the risk of provocation, to be weary of what women, especially educated women, tell him they want. They will at once say they want an equal and a partner, somebody sensitive and nurturing. They want somebody somewhat less masculine, and less prone to bursts of testosterone-fueled behavior. And yet as you go into the world you will find that women do NOT really want this man. They want a Man. They want everything.

What I perceive in Muppets From Space is a warning to men that they should be aware to some extent of the female guile and wiles. There is all too great a danger of becoming feminized, and a feminized masculinity is by no means what the future needs. Truth is a woman, Nietzsche said, and can only ever love a warrior. Do not be submissive, and do not let a woman convince you your masculine tendencies are primitive or barbaric. They are a spiritual force of great use, and a woman who wants to deplete that well is a succubus, no doubt.

Yes, we are supposed to root for Miss Piggy, and her emasculation does lead her to COVNET. This is something. If thematically this is what occurring, than certainly COVNET must represent the result of a masculine and hyper-rationalistic and violent world, as we've already noted.

Without going as far as some critics, we must accept that the modern world was built in man's image. To certain feministic thinkers, everything from the shape of our skyscrapers to the design of our missiles is phallic.

Heed me though, young gentleman – the typical woman will become dissatisfied with the soft-souled man she in fact created. It's a vicious cycle, but I have seen it regularly.

Miss Piggy and the Man In Black. She wants to get the scoop. Bondage, power, sexes. The feminine to get at the truth by bonding the masculine.

***

The dark irony is that the only character holding faith in Gonzo is Singer, his alleged nemesis. Of course, we adventurers in film theory already know these two are doppelgangers, each one a side of a two-faced coin. After a slaphappy appearance on a popular news program, alerting Singer to Gonzo's existence, Gonzo is picked up by two dark-suited, sun-glass wearing men, the famous Men In Black. By promising to put Gonzo in contact with his people, he and Rizzo are tricked into entering the very bowels of COVNET itself.

At this point Singer confronts Gonzo for the first time. After preparing Gonzo in a high chair for a rude and hostile interrogation, Singer explains his identification with Gonzo as one who is alone in the world and laughed at by others.

Singer's fascination with Gonzo is singular. He has been waiting his entire life to confront such a being. He slips on a rubber glove to touch and examine the Muppet. He wants to maintain a medical and scientific distance between them, a barrier synonymous with nothing more than sterility. Singer has a disgusted fascination with Gonzo.
There is a reference to proctology here, as Singer asks Gonzo if he minds, and Rizzo recommends asking about the destination of that finger.

After twisting on his beak and pushing his nose back, Singer notes that Gonzo has no nostrils and asks, How do you smell?

Rizzo offers, Awful, trust me, I'm his roommate.

As they all crack up, Singer bursts into an apoplectic rage. DON'T LAUGH AT ME! He screams. Everyone is of course surprised at the outburst, and more than a little disturbed.

Forgive me my Earthly manners, but do you have any idea what it's like to be laughed at? Sure enough, Gonzo does.

To be called names like wacko and freak boy?

And paranoid delusional psychopath?

Gonzo says, You got me there.

To feel completely alone in this world? Singer asks.

Rizzo stops him there, saying, Yeah, I think we're starting to get the general idea there, Ed. At this moment Rizzo becomes very uncomfortable with the direction of the conversation.

But wouldn't it have been interesting to see where the questioning went? To see what we could learn about the dualistic relationship between Gonzo and Singer?

It is clear that both of them have taken different approaches to the same threats against life.

Though Gonzo relates at first, Singer continues to we find that Gonzo and Singer have branched off in their approaches.

Do you have any

Gonzo has responded to modern malaise with a deep spiritual sadness and longing for wholeness. Singer has succumbed to aggressive, paranoiac hatred of the Other. Singer wants Gonzo to reveal the plans of the alien beings trying to locate him, about which Gonzo quite honestly denies any knowledge. Incredulous, Singer arranges for the removal of Gonzo's brain. There is general protest, but it is taken care of by the cameo appearance of a singular American icon, Hollywood Hulk Hogan. But this time he is dressed all in back and is working for the bad guys instead of looking out for the underdog.

The Bear acts surprised, "Wrestling legend Hollywood Hulk Hogan?" Why is there such a need to

This is for all my NWOites out there. I will continue to dominate wrestling. He goes on to assure us that he will makes our backs crack, our knees freeze, and our livers quiver. He will continue to put so much pain on you that you will become his painiac. Before Hogan dumps Rizzo into the chute that will take him to the basement laboratory, Rizzo asks what his fans are going to think. Hogan shrugs and says he is a bad guy now. He has gone from All-American to Hollywood. As Hollywood, he leads a group called the New World Order, which is most important.

There is many levels on which this is relevant. First and foremost, it is important thematically to the film to recognize that nationalism may not be the answer to the world's pressing problems. As a soft nationalist, it takes some prodding to accept this.

But what we also see is the falseness of media personalities as role models. This may be a banal observation by now, but the importance of this fact, and its implications, are extremely important to consider. Just because we recognize that the human stars behind popular characters have nothing to do with one another, doesn't mean that this dissonance ceases to have profound ramifications.

Sticking Hollywood Hulk Hogan into the film at this juncture was either a move of the grossest inanity and shortsightedness, or the greatest consideration and foresight. It is easy to look at the appearance of this wrestler-cum-thespian as a crass, shameless resort to celebrity endorsement and cameo. Why, after all, should this man be placed here, in this film, at this particular juncture? Our first instinct may be to dismiss the cameo as poor planning, even some kind of obligatory bone tossed to the studios. Did they, for instance, have a contract with Hulk Hogan? Was he promised a moment in one of their films, and did it matter which one, or whether it was relevant to the story being told? Hollywood Hulk Hogan even goes into a monologue.

I myself prefer to argue a different theory. To say it once more: in a film as tightly constructed as *Muppets From Space*, one has to assume every minor event, much less every major event, has a specific and thoughtfully rendered relationship to the whole. Especially one as jarring as an apparently moronic decision to cast Hollywood Hulk Hogan as himself. We are fortunate as analysts who believe in Muppets From Space to find many gains by casting Hulk Hogan.

First Possibility With Hulk Hogan: I am not against the possibility Hulk Hogan was brought in just to tear down the Fourth Wall between performer and audience. This would have been done to sharply remind the viewer that though he is watching a work of fiction, the same dynamics seen within are those operating in the real world outside the movie theater. To momentarily yank a viewer out of suspended disbelief makes him consider what he is viewing from a more complex approach. In short, *Muppets From Space* is conscious of itself as Art in its most profound sense.

Additionally, the fact that forty years from now nobody will know who Hulk Hogan is, thus rendering his cameo in the movie completely void of its amusement factor, demonstrates the piercing vision the creators have of their own commercial art. Basically they are telling us that in a society like ours, where even art, religion, spirituality, and the family have become commodities, *Muppets From Space* will be as good as obliterated when it is buried beneath the avalanche of popular culture. Think about it: Howdy Doody. How many kids know who the fuck Howdy Doody is? That shit was from the 1950's when television channels numbered about thirteen.

But today, there is a different icon on every one of a thousand television stations, and so America can no longer remember any favorite icon together as a nation. In ten years, when we say *The Grinch*, people will ask us if we mean the Jim Carrey movie. I don't know about you, but I'm just old enough to vaguely recall when *Starsky & Hutch* was still syndicated on network television, but still young enough to have no idea what it was about the show the recent movie starring Ben Stiller and Luke Wilson was sending up. Bill Watterson, the creator of *Calvin & Hobbes*, will be forgotten. He never sold out and he never sold the movie rights, so to speak. All *Calvin & Hobbes* merchandise is bootleg and unofficial. Jim Davis, the creator of the abominable Garfield will probably always be remembered.

So by insisting on this cameo, the directors have subtly informed us art itself, even beloved art like *Muppets From Space*, is just grist for the mill in a consumer society. Companies will need new Muppet stories in the future, because they will always need to make money, or different versions of Muppets when the Muppets can no longer get people into theaters. We might even say here that Hulk Hogan's constant reappearance and recreation, like Madonna's, is representative of how corporate culture operates. Professional wrestling needed to make money and appeal to audiences who were older, and they did not have the imagination to invent new ways, so they had to rehash an old one, Hulk Hogan.

Always bank on what has succeeded before, that is a sensible business motto. Only Hogan needed to be transformed, so they turned him into Hollywood Hulk Hogan. And folks, to be honest I have no fucking clue who Hollywood Hulk Hogan is or what his character is supposed to remind us of. Old Hulk Hogan used to mean something, I guess. But I have no associations with this Hollywood Hulk.

But ironically, what the creators have also accomplished by cementing their film into history—historicizing and dating it—is to have sent a message to the future; shot it ahead fifty or a hundred years as if blasted out of a time-cannon. In some dark dystopian future, where we have become complete drones of the corporate media and capitalist infrastructure, movies will be so sophisticated that not even one potentially thought-provoking idea will be included in them. Nothing that might disturb the social or economic order. Just as is done with our so-called "transgressive" art today, every potentially provocative idea will be neutralized from its cooption and assimilation by the economic system. Scarlet Johansson, Woody Allen, Jamie Foxx, Jake Gyllenhaal, Sean Penn, Tim Robbins, Susan Sarandon, and others who believe they are actually making art and not propaganda which serves to buttress a certain economic system will still make irreverent, critically acclaimed films and be quoted in magazines expressing controversial ideas, only they will do so as animated characters, just as "real" as the real thing. People will not know the difference, even at public and red-carpet appearances, due to advancements in hologram technology. Cameos will not be done by real men and women, people who live and die and go the way of all flesh. They will be animated icons, so realistic that one cannot tell the difference between them and a human icon. When the thematic or marketing elements call for a cameo, these icons will be digitally inserted into the film. These icons will span generations, and will in effect be eternal. But in all of this simulation, there may come a Messiah. And he may find a copy of *Muppets From Space* in his great-grandfather's chest up in the attic. He may find a television/DVD player combination in there as well. And he may fire it up and look at a time in the glorious past when real entertainers made real cameos. He may realize that he doesn't know this person Hulk Hogan, but that there was a time in history when people were expected to. This may clue him in to how relevance is maintained in the culture industry of his own day. And he may end up being the leader of a revolutionary resistance by humans against the domination of machines. Maybe his name will be John Conner, maybe it won't. But what is certain is that the resistance will succeed, and cameos will once again be made by real humans. In light of this, we see that the creators of this film saw their movie not only as relevant art, but as the manual of revolution for a distant age. The last hope for humanity in a stark, dystopian future.

All this is fodder for future commentators and analysts. So what about for those of us living today? Where is our bone? Where is our explanation for Hulk Hogan's appearance in the film? After all, the appearance of *any* celebrity playing him or herself self would have broached the Fourth Wall. Having not paid attention to professional wrestling since I was five years old, I don't know what associations the younger generation has with the star. I would think anybody younger than me would have an even more diluted association with Hulk Hogan. They might be vaguely cognizant of his existence, but would he have any more associations attached to him? Keep in mind, this cameo was long before the Hulk's reality show, which though I never saw, I now associate with him.

But I believe the decision to cast Hogan was made not because of his identity as Hollywood Hulk Hogan, but because of his decades-old persona as Mister America, the Real American. Now, in association with the paranoiac defense group COVNET, he is a bad guy, and admits as much. This shows the viewer that America can in fact act evil in the name of its security, and to be on guard against those tendencies. If America often fights for freedom and the good cause, it also occasionally puts Japanese people in internment camps and goes to war for the sake of corporate profits. (This example to be considered outside the actual debate over Japanese internment camps, and is merely to stress that every nation has acted cruelly and unmercifully in support of causes later generations deem unjust, having the benefit of hindsight). The message is that what occurs in the name of national security does not always occur beyond good and evil.

Gonzo is further interrogated by Singer, but cannot answer any of Singer's questions. Who are they? Where do they come from? When will they arrive? What for Gonzo is hope of redemption stokes fear in Singer. His intentions have moved outward. Instead of Who am I, he asks who they are. Instead of where do I come from, where do they come from?

Both Gonzo and Singer are anxious for the arrival. But because Singer feels the urgency, he cannot wait for Gonzo to be in touch down the road. He sends Gonzo to have his brain removed.

Meanwhile, Rizzo has shot down the shoot into a cage full of fellow rats. After meeting the other inmates, he is told they are lab rats. In keeping with Rizzo as a mere sensualist, and spirit of mediocre rank, we can draw a few conclusions. His travels down the tube are also a kind of birth, and in the end he is born into a prison. His fate here reminds us of nothing so much as the famous story of Plato's Cave.

Rizzo's prison mates are all rats.

This is the suggestion that the Rat Race is a prison.

Rizzo at first tries to maintain his humanity by cracking a joke about eating. The jest doesn't go over well with Dr. Tucker, played to perfection by David Arquette.

While there he runs into a Mengeles character named Dr. Tucker, portrayed to the fullest by that old scene-stealer David Arquette. David Arquette: the A stands for always breathtaking, the I for infinitely talented.

It is one of the film's masterstrokes to cast David Arquette, or as we film theorists know him, The David. Few other actors would have been capable of combining both the sadistic and comedic elements of an inuman biological researcher in such perfect harmony. It is this kind of work which informed his inspired role as an Elvis impersonator in *3000 Miles to Graceland* and the unforgettable Shark Boy in the film *Shark Boy and Lava Girl.* The immensity of talent in the Arquette family leaves one astounded, and one wishes prayer were actually efficacious, so that one might pray they all continue to make the fascinating films they do.

Arquette's Dr. Tucker is of course symbolic of both Science-As-God and the Banality of Evil, best represented by the mundane Nazi bureaucracy which was responsible for heaping so many terrors upon the human spirit. The Nazis forced us to ask ourselves whether or not any of us, given the right circumstances, might be capable of similar atrocities. Science divorced from human compassion has given the world a great deal of suffering. But there is more.

It is medical science in particular that comes under attack. COVNET is clearly not just a bureau for tracking extraterrestrial threats, but is an underground but tacitly authorized research facility. Tucker is both a doctor and a jailer-torturer, a sadistic scientist whose pursuit of knowledge has taken him beyond the confines of morality. A sociopathic villain, he is incapable of experiencing empathy for the Other. His punishment of his subjects is putting them in the maze, but these exercises will also be studies which will benefit mankind, and even perhaps animal-kind—is he hero or villain or some toxic mix of both? That Arquette plays Tucker so ambiguously is another bell tolled to announce his genius to the very Heavens.

Is he a caricature set up to poke fun at naïve hippie stereotypes about the bio-medical researcher? Or is he in fact an amplification of real tendencies in the researchers at these laboratories? Aye, but Tucker is *both* simultaneously, as Arquette must consciously and brilliantly have played him, and thereby the character stubbornly refuses to reveal his true nature to us, though we subject him to every form of conceptual analysis, the way he subjects his rats to every kind of agonizing study.

It is instructive that Rizzo is a true prisoner.

"Nobody has escaped from the maze!" Tucker screams maniacally. Indeed, nobody can escape the complex maze of Arquette's perfectly balanced and intricate performance. But what he means is that nobody escapes the maze, or prison, of the modern world. What redeems us destroys us, what gives us happiness creates despair, what solves our problems creates more problems. We humans too have been compared convincingly to rats in a maze, or competitors in a "rat race." And even if this comparison now seems to us unimaginative and clichéd, it is apt to a disheartening degree.

A maze is of enormous symbooism. The funk song playing is Survival of the Fittest.

While awaiting his brain removal surgery in a holding cell, Gonzo is brought a sandwich. Gonzo sets the meal aside and ere long it begins speaking to him. Like the alphabet cereal, this food item is somehow conveying the transmissions from Gonzo's kin. A peculiar move, and the adventurer in film theory is prone to ask, why a talking sandwich? Is it mere gimmickry? Arbitrary? But if nothing in this film is arbitrary, as is clearly the case, it is precisely here that we must grab our spades and dig deep. For this scene we could have witnessed nearly any speaking snack, but a sandwich was chosen, and it must be explained. Just as there were reasons for choosing the alphabet cereal, a sandwich is rich with analytical possibility.

It is common knowledge that John Montagu, Earl of Sandwich, was responsible for the meal that bears his namesake; however, this is really common *prejudice*. Montagu did indeed popularize the sandwich. His slab of meat between two slices of bread caught on in a big way as a convenient meal on the go for a busy noble. But Montagu is by no means to be credited with its invention. The first recorded sandwich in history was the creation of Hillel the Elder, a famous Jewish religious scholar from the first century BC.

Hillel was frequently found piling the Paschal lamb and bitter herbs of the Jewish Seder between two pieces of matzo, in what turned out to be a most delicious Jewish treat. The ingredients of the Jewish Seder are meant to evoke associations with Exodus, when the Hebrews escaped from their slavery and servitude to the Egyptians, and particularly that nasty despot the Pharaoh. It is thus apropos that a sandwich above all other snacks would do the talking here. Gonzo himself requires a similar Exodus: both physically from COVNET, and from the spiritual vacuum of modern secular society. The militarized and industrial world is like the metropolis of ancient Egypt. As an example of organized public works, Egypt was a marvel, as are our modern societies. And yet there will always be those who feel oppressed by its majesty. There is a Pharaoh inside every one of us, who will not let us go, who is afraid and resentful. We must overcome this Pharaoh.

Interestingly, Hillel the Elder is thought to have been born thirty to sixty years before the birth of Jesus, and to have died when Jesus was about ten years old. Thus he spans the transition from a pagan/Judaic world into the world of Christendom.

Hillel had two famous quotes, both of which are relevant to the themes of *Muppets From Space*. The first is, "If I am not for myself, who will be? If I am only for myself, what am I? And if not now, when?" What these words suggest for Gonzo is that he and he alone is capable of overcoming his spiritual malaise, and he cannot rely on the teachings or spiritual tenacity of others. Yet, love and care for others is essential to any human interested in living a meaningful life and enjoying a rich, fulfilling existence—certainly within the Muppet world, if not reality itself. And lastly, this change in us should take place immediately. There is no reason to procrastinate or put it off. These matters of the spirit are always urgent, regardless of the age we live in. We know not the day nor the hour of our death, and our lives can indeed be seen as a spiritual quest.

Hillel's second famous quote occurred after a man, very short on time we assume, challenged him to explain the meaning of the Torah, all while standing on one leg. Hillel lifted his leg and explained, "That which is hateful to you, do not do to your fellow. That is the whole Torah; the rest is the explanation; go and learn." Thus Hillel anticipated Jesus' own formulation of The Golden Rule by thirty or forty years: "Do unto others as you would have them do unto you." The Golden Rule is perhaps the most common ethical observance or recommendation, and is formulated in every one of the world's major religions. It also has parallels in pagan ethical codes as well, such as Aristotle's *Nichomachean Ethics* and Epicurus' moral prescriptions.

In deciphering how the famous tenet relates to *Muppets From Space*, we must see The Golden Rule as protection against becoming monsters in the service of some bureaucracy or institution, putting the interests of an impersonal code of conduct above love and concern for our fellow man. The Nazi bureaucracy was able to initiate extermination of the Jews because each individual within the mechanics of the bureaucracy was able to shift the blame from himself to that of an institution wherein no one person shouldered the responsibility. The Nazi's were not monsters as such. They were people like you and I, under an authoritative rule that condoned such actions.

Indeed, research into social psychology indicates that most all of us would inflict suffering on another person if an "authority" pressures us into doing so. But if we can empathize with the Other, we can free ourselves from the dehumanization of modern social organization, and like a French and German soldier dying together in a WWI trench, reach across the muck and mud and recognize the humanity of one another.
And yet, what we will see by the end of the film is that it is really in one another that we find salvation. More on that later, but there are clues throughout that this is the solution the film is building towards. There are certainly valid critiques

of this solution, and we will get to those when the time comes.

The sandwich first tells Gonzo they would like to meet him at his home. Gonzo is opposed to this because the personnel at COVNET are aware of the location. It would be thematically inconsistent were they to meet at Gonzo's home, precisely because Gonzo's home is merely a house. Gonzo needs what is new and novel. He needs to escape home in order that he might transcend the circumstances of his birth and his

Instead of his home, Gonzo recommends they meet at Cape Doom at midnight. Surely such a foreboding name for their landing point is no accident. Here will be the final showdown where man will either triumph by thrusting himself into the next higher plane of spiritual, psychological and social awareness—or be destroyed. If not destroyed outright, he will hence be "doomed" to remain locked, or arrested, in this unhealthy and unwholesome stage of spiritual development. Man shall then forever remain an empty shell of his former self, a husk, a fallen ruin.

That Gonzo is to be there at midnight suggests the finality of this showdown, where all will be decided from here to the end of man's duration as a species. Midnight is 12 o'clock, and 12 o'clock is High Noon, the time when gunslingers meet in the dusty streets to engage in battle and do death's work. There can be no compromises in gun-slinging. One man's fate is to die, the other's to live. The potential man of the future will either live or die on the shores of Cape Doom, while the sickly man of today will do the same. The two cannot co-exist. Midnight is the High Noon in the dark night of man's soul. But we are permitted to maintain cautious hope, for as is said, the darkest hour is right before the dawn.

While Gonzo converses with his sandwich, Kermit and the gang are making preparations for a daring rescue. The group has consulted their resident scientists, Beaker and Dr. Honeydew, in order to gain some technical assistance. This assistance comes in the form of a few clever gadgets. Ironically, here we see science helping to rescue Gonzo from an oppressive technocracy. Technology of course can be wielded by massive institutions and bureaucracies, and their impersonal machinations may imprison us in a cell, whether we are speaking of imprisonment of the body or of the mind. But technology at a more grassroots, independent level can be the very tool which aids us in our escape from modernity. Especially when wielded by community members who have a stake, or at least feel they have a stake, in the health and happiness of the community at large.

A multinational mega-corporation would not have the community's mental and physical well-being in mind when thinking about its technological innovations; however a smaller scale business or industry just might, and certainly most of our greatest scientists do. As social and regional mobility fragments and scatters our communities, peppering their members to locales spanning the entire globe, we are in danger of losing the very existence of community, and even the very concept itself. True, there may come a time when the entire world and its ecosystem appears to us as our community. But it may also be that a proper sense of community on this kind of massive scale can only be imaginary and delusional, probably forced onto us from above by an economic system that *requires*—and thus *demands*—our mobility and detachment. Thus the only truly meaningful social ties would be local.

Of particular interest to us are the devices the Muppets are given. The first of these is a rubber duck which also happens to eject an invisibility spray.

The third device is a rubber duck that sprays invisibility spray. Its effects are temporary. We must first ask, what is the meaning of invisibility in this film? And secondly, why must this power come from a rubber duck? Invisibility is required for the group to sneak into and then sneak around COVNET. But the invisibility soon wears off before the Muppets even have time to locate Gonzo. This fact itself deserves countless volumes of conceptual unpacking and theoretical extrapolation. But briefly, we must become invisible to COVNET before we can infiltrate it.

When you are protected from the repercussions of knowing and criticizing the Social System, you will be granted the freedom necessary to understanding and exploring it. For instance, Christianity could never have been toppled while it was still thought to be capable of peering into your soul, or of using real force against you in the real world. I say toppled even though Christianity is alive and well, because the creed of Christianity has been toppled for a long time, even if the religion lives on.

It was also the institution holding the keys to your salvation and securing you a decent afterlife. Not to mention you probably actually believed in Christianity, as many people still do. But so long as the Church wielded real and unchecked political power, these roadblocks to true understanding remained in place, and there could never have been an honest analysis of the religion. It simply wouldn't have been feasible. Even the most intellectually courageous and daring men and women between the day of Christ's crucifixion and the first stirrings of the Enlightenment were forced to bend over backwards in what today we see as embarrassing prostration to the Church.

It was almost 1700 years until Christianity could be reasonably assessed by rival creeds such as Deism, popularized by John Locke. And it would be another fifty years before it could be attacked from the vantage point of atheism, of whom the first modern example is Baron d'Holbach, who must have been a very courageous man indeed.

A famous quote of Baron d'Holbach's is relevant, so I shall here reproduce it at length:

"If we go back to the beginning we shall find that ignorance and fear created the gods; that fancy, enthusiasm, or deceit adorned or disfigured them; that weakness worships them; that credulity preserves them, and that custom, respect and tyranny support them in order to make the blindness of men serve its own interests."

Though the Baron was talking about supernaturalism and the Church, the last phrase says that the blindness of men aids Tyranny in forcing men to serve the interest of Tyranny. Capitalist Society, or whatever we call the world we live in today, blinds us in order that we may serve its interests. Now, in a Capitalistic Society the interests of the dominating institutions ideally harmonize with the interests of the people, but this is not always the case, and institutions designed to aid men in their search for happiness often take on a life and momentum all their own, often becoming free from our oversight and control.

COVNET has the upper hand in this particular battle because COVNET is Technocracy itself, and as such COVNET has designed the very world we live, work, and play in, arguably going all the way back to the first townships and civilizations. It is COVNET's world, we just live in it. So in order to orient ourselves with COVNET, it must become blind to us, thereby losing its firm grip upon our psyches, thought patterns, and conceptual prejudices. Of course this invisibility can only be a temporary state. Simply recognizing the truth about the organization of our society does not free us from it. Everybody still must live in the same world when tomorrow comes. And yet, go live in the mountains where the marketers and media people cannot reach you. Stay there for a long time. Then come back to civilization—you will realize that they do not even know how to speak to you any more. And why should they? After all, they no longer know you.

That the invisibility spray is squirted from a duck is also a detail worthy of the attention of a hundred scholars, or a thousand. The rubber duck is a highly enigmatic symbol, yet we are not without the keys to at least a few of its hidden doorways and secret passages. In fact, the rubber duck is far more popular as a symbolic device than most people realize.

Especially, it makes appearances in many popular science fiction and fantasy films. Refer to Wikipedia if you would like to see but a fraction of the list.

The popularity of the rubber duck in science fiction and fantasy is due to two things. Firstly because of that old phrase: if it looks like a duck, quacks like a duck, and swims like a duck, then it is a duck. But that line holds less true today than it ever did, although it has always been subject to philosophical critique. For example, how do know it is a duck? Perhaps there is an evil demon who has some obscure motive for making me believe it really is a duck when in fact it is not a duck. One way of accomplishing this would be for the evil demon to make it appear to my senses that it is a duck. Or course, to convince me absolutely he would also have to convince me my senses were not subject to error, and we're not sure whether or not this hypothetical demon has that much power or develops his strategy for deception with that contingency in mind.

Secondly, we must recall that one of the major problems of modernity is the Self. Remember *Bladerunner*, the movie starring Harrison Ford, directed by Ridley Scott, and based on the novel by Phillip Dick? Simulation—and simulacra—were the major themes of both the book and the movie. What is simulacra? Well, suppose the existence of a life-like bio-mechanical robot made to resemble a duck in almost every way. Suppose it even looks like a duck, quacks like a duck, and swims like a duck. Yet, knowing it is not a duck, we would have to oppose common sense and conclude it is something other than a duck. It is simulacra, because it shares all the characteristics which go into making a duck a duck, a yet it is not a duck but something else.

Now that we can biologically clone organisms, thus bio-chemical "androids," we still cannot even say whether or not some thing which is the exact re-creation of some other thing is still a distinct thing, conceptually speaking. And of course, if a computer program exhibits with absolute convincingness all the behaviors of human sentience, by what rationale could we not accord it the status of a person?

So simulacra, even though they create a serious crisis for mankind, also present him with an opportunity to reshape himself, by seeing that the definition of the human is never firmly set in stone. The existence of simulacra has thus forced us into seeking a definition for ourselves, but to do that we must clear away the baggage of society and history as far as we can, and for that we must be invisible. It might also be said that the duck is considered the most laughable and ridiculous of all birds, mostly due to the waddling, clumsy way it walks and the heavy, ponderous way it flies. This advises us that we should not fear becoming ridiculous or a buffoon or an object of laughter, because such experiments may in the end prove to be the most fruitful for our explorations. A certain sense of merry buffoonery may in fact be the first characteristic we include in a realistic and workable definition of the human. Indeed, the Muppets themselves are just such buffoons.

     is an aerosol spray that allows the sprayer to control the mind of whoever is sprayed. This is wielding the weapon of modern mass media—only possible through advanced technology—against itself. Because we can hardly remove ourselves from the profound influence of mass media, we might well imagine that most of our thoughts and opinions, if not all of them, are shaped directly by it or in response to it, attributing to ourselves hypothetical degrees of autonomy based on our level of paranoia concerning whether we really are who we think we are, or do *they* just make us think we are who we are.

Of course individuals can never mold the public mind the way a media conglomerate can, but on a more intimate one-to-one level, we possess an equal power; and *Muppets From Space* would suggest we hold more than equal power. So by spraying the guard (Ray Liotta), at the front gate of COVNET, as Miss Piggy will do later, she displaces his bureaucratic brainwashing and he is compelled to let the rescuers pass freely through the barrier.

One might Miss Piggy of merely engaging in another form of brainwashing, and that her actions are morally no different than those of COVNET's. But I tend to favor a different interpretation. No, Miss Piggy did not free Liotta from his regimented internalization of COVNET's values. No, she did not turn him into an utterly autonomous moral being. No he did not make the self-determined decision to allow the Muppets passage from some superlatively independent, detached vantage point completely free of social context. But I would argue that is entirely the point of the scene.

There is so much belief these days in "independent thought," we don't even see that independent thought as such is impossible. There has never been a thought in the history of humankind that was not based on some prior thought. Art builds on art, and Newton stood on the shoulders of giants. What we actually mean by independent thought is that somebody thoroughly considers evidence for a position and makes a reasonable decision to either make that position his own or to scorn it as utter falsity. But his decision was made within a context of available information, a moral conscience, and a social conscience. There is no thought whatsoever in a social vacuum.

In fact, this blindness to the social foundation for all states of mind, especially our ethical ones, may be a technique employed by the System to atomize us for convenient exploitation. This is not to advocate entirely for the side of social nature in arriving at conclusions. Indeed, a society dominated by human groupthink would probably be far worse than one dominated by the institutional groupthink necessary to Technocracy, and certainly more full of cruelty and violence. But we must still escape from this sense of being an isolated mind whose thoughts and beliefs are not simultaneously the mirror *of* and the mirroring *for* another human being's thoughts and beliefs. Truth, as is practically self-evident, can only be a group phenomenon.

The second piece of techno-wizardry is a jar of jelly that, when tossed on a wall, creates a doorway. The doorway it creates turns out to be a very small one most everybody in the group cannot fit through, but luckily Pepe the Prawn is just the right size. After traveling through, he winds up opening a different door on the opposite wall of the corridor, thus allowing the group to escape COVNET. Of course the jar of jelly represents fruit that has undergone the scientific manufacturing process, and thereby a natural piece of Earth becomes part of the fabricated, artificial world of humans. The fruit is the processed version of the "Forbidden Fruit" that Adam and Eve ate in the Garden.

The discussion of the allegorical meaning of the fruit was touched on elsewhere, and was associated with the forbidden fruit of knowledge, which thrusts us up into new levels of consciousness which can be disorienting and frightening. But here the leap of consciousness is to be *out* of something frightening—namely, the realities of Technocratic Society—into an unknown future, whereas the prior leap in consciousness was from a state of pacified unknowing into our present jumble of turbulent realization.

Though it cannot be certain that the future is rosy, we at least have a fifty-fifty chance that it will be better than the world we live in today. Those are good odds to bet on, because we know the world of today is a full 100% devastating to the soul of man. We may be able to live better, longer, healthier, happier lives, but this freedom and health has led to greater, more intensive searching for the human Self, which cannot be discovered while we are still in the throes of modernity. But the doorway is small, and the vast majority will not make it through without the assistance of small numbers of exceptional people leading the way.

If we are to see these gadgets as symbolically representing the tools we need in coming to terms with our society, we need to place them in the order they are used, because it is different from the order in which they are presented to us by Beaker and Honeydew in the lab. First the spray is used, implying we must first recognize the social nature and public utility of all ethics and world-views. Secondly, the invisible spray is used. This implies we must then become invisible to Technocracy—in a sense, momentarily free from the passive absorption of its value system so that we are free to explore it objectively and without interference. Lastly, we must not be afraid of dashing old ways against the wall, because by their breakage new doors will be opened up, and these doors just may lead to new forms of escape.

On their way to COVNET Doctor Beaker and Doctor Bunsen Honeydew are accidentally left at the gas station. This is to indicate that science and technology will not themselves be the weapons that win the day against COVNET, but will provide the necessary assistance. And science, or more properly Scientism, can be neglected after having served its purpose. The solution to our problems will include a blending of science and human irrationality, logic and emotion, fact and fantasy—all of them being so very necessary to our happiness and to a world we could consider fit for human habitation. Irrationality will be used.

Before we continue it will be necessary to mention the scenes involving the actress Kathy Griffin. Griffin is not, like David Arquette, a thespian of almost religious brilliance, but here she may as well be considered as such. Griffin plays a female guard at COVNET, one who comes upon the Muppets in their attempts to rescue and escape with Gonzo.

Fozzie washes his hands after using the bathroom. Just after the Muppet's invisibility spray wears off she comes around the corner. At first ready to blast the group with her pistol, she lays eyes on Animal. His role in the rescue, then—which hasn't been clear until now—is to seduce Griffin, creating a window of time for the rest of the group to accomplish the task at hand. We must ask ourselves three questions. First, Who is Animal the Muppet? Second, Who is the human Kathie Griffin? And thirdly, why does their coming together in sexual union have thematic importance within the film, especially as regards her allowance of the group to continue unimpeded on their rescue mission?

To begin, we have a pretty clear idea who Animal is. His creator Frank Oz has been quoted as saying he winnowed the character of Animal down to five words: Sex, Sleep, Food, Drums and Pain. Animal, thus, represents the "animalistic" aspects of humankind. Some would call him a slacker, but he is really a very intense specialist—like Frank Oz in the creation of him, he has winnowed his life pursuits down to the very basics, the elementals, and has cast off whatever else as so much dead weight. He is not a brilliant religious theorist, but like a Buddhist monk, his focus is dramatic. He wants to bang on drums like a primitive, sleep in late like a primitive, and eat like a primitive. He wants to experience pain and sex like a primitive.

In short, Animal is the caveman women so often crave. He exudes raw sexuality and sensuality, but while also maintaining his feminine sensitivity (he is an artist), and devotion to his calling, which is fundamentally creative. He is dangerous but he is not so dangerous that he is a sociopath, without receptivity to female emotions.

But if the light shed on Animal is bright, it is dim on Kathy Griffin. Who is this enigmatic woman? I would posit that she is symbolic of mankind's ultimate corruption, its ability to sell itself out for the sake of base sensual pleasures. In this way she is the ultimate temptress, a whore of Babylon, a deceiver sent to cloud the eyes of men through her feminine wiles. The genius of Griffin in this film, though, is not attributable to her as an actor—but rather, to one of those unsung heroes of the film industry, the Casting Director. There is nothing in Griffin's depiction of the female security guard that we can consider artful. In fact, friends—and this analytical tool is absolutely essential to the contemporary film theorist: What Kathy Griffin represents in *real life* is what Kathy Griffin represents in the character of Female Guard (the title of her role).

So what does Kathy Griffin represent in real life? To begin with, she is famous for being a mediocrity, which she gladly acknowledges. Her routine is almost completely composed of gibes at more important entertainers from the vantage point of a "D-List celebrity." Secondly, she is partially blind due to a bumbled LASIK surgery, and often rails against LASIK—thus she uses her own blindness as an excuse to stress to others the importance of remaining blind.

Because she is blind, she feels that everybody else should also be blind, and her perfect revenge would be to stab the eyes out of all who see clearly. She is a militant atheist who wants to be a Unitarian—meaning, her belief in nothing leads her to desire a creed wherein everybody's beliefs are validated and none too harshly criticized. Her act also consists of pointing out the decadent behavior of celebrities in the entertainment industry, mostly those associated with Hollywood—drug abuse, promiscuity, alcoholism, religious cults, and so on. In so doing she paints a pastiche of the utter nihilism found behind the scenes of the world's most popular and influential art form, the film.

Like painfully unfunny comedienne Margaret Cho, she has a huge gay following, and her act often panders to that audience's particular humor and interests. She calls these fans "my gays." Thus she inadvertently endorses infertility as a good, which is contrary to the basic drive found in all of life. In particular she endorses human infertility. And lastly, she is an avowed teetotaler who does not drink alcohol. But if she does not promote ecstatic "loss-of-self" through the use of intoxicating spirits, does she promote finding that loss-of-self through some other method? Yes, she says food is her "vice," in lieu of alcohol, cigarettes, or drugs. As such she is the very model of a typical feminine response to depression and despair—she eats. But because food does not intoxicate, its operations as a vice are quite unique.

A woman eats and then becomes guilty about putting on weight, which makes her eat more. It's a vicious cycle, one in which the submersion into despair and guilt become as gratifying psychologically as the food. And perhaps in more morbid dispositions the food was always a mere vehicle to the guilt-cycle. In this way, overeating performs like passion and sin in romantic Catholicism, wherein the sinner loves to sin so that he can experience the orgasmic bliss of redemption through Christ's forgiveness.

Griffin, as we said, encounters the Muppets just moments after they regain visibility.

Nietzsche said, Going to see woman? Bring a whip. Animal is the masculine energy needed to tame the female.

Remember, invisibility is what allowed them to freely explore COVNET as Technocracy. We also said their regaining visibility was to demonstrate that understanding Technocracy does not thereby free us from it. For many people this realization is the moment they begin to give up hope, and fall into nihilistic despair. The system seems too powerful to overcome. And in the end we do not even know whether any other system could be better, seeing as how this system at least successfully secures the basics of happiness for large numbers of people. The basics of happiness being food, shelter, and security.

This is the moment of greatest danger for those who gravitate towards higher states of spiritual existence. Seeing that all is in vain, they become hedonists. Not in the classical sense, but in the modern sense. The difference is easy to illustrate. Take as an example the online magazine devoted to sensuality and palate, *Epicurious*, put out by the dunderheads at Conde Nast. Epicurus is considered the founder of hedonism because he advocated for the pursuit of pleasure as the highest good. But his pleasure was friends, peacefulness, and philosophical contemplation. He lived on a diet of bread and water.

Today most hedonists do not find pleasure in philosophical contemplation, though they may pretend to so they can seem intelligent and "deep" to their peers, whether it be fellow dramatic arts students at NYU, fellow twerps at faggot-ass hipster clubs on the Lower East Side, or the "artists" in the entertainment industry. What hedonists take pleasure in today is what used to be considered debauchery. Fornication and whoredom are two more apt descriptors.

And whether art imitates life or life imitates art, the debauchery of those who work in the entertainment industry, and the debauchery of much of the entertainment itself, shows us where we are and where we are headed. And when many of the most influential people seek escape into every kind of sensual oblivion, where we are headed is over the brink of Nihilism Canyon. Just like those two bitches in *Thelma & Louise*. So here comes Griffin, who falls in "lust" with Animal.

Certain ridiculous women ascribe to "sex" as such the role of empowerment device. They say one empowers oneself by disassociating guilt or public utility from the sexual act, and indulging your "natural instincts." Has there ever been some dumb cunt starlet who said sex is sacred and should only be participated in by two people committed fully to one another's well-being and care? If so, I've never heard about it. Nietzsche said that the kind and quality of a person's sexuality reaches up into the very pinnacle of their being. If he is correct, than our cultural obsession with self-indulgent licentiousness—particularly the sexual obsession displayed by political and social liberals—implies a nation who is fast losing any sense of purpose or meaning.

The release of *Girls Gone Wild* and the first print-run of *Maxim* magazine might then be considered the tolling of the bell which signaled our death (which may not have come yet even though it has already arrived). The "skipping towards Gomorra" attitude of liberals would be the nails in our coffin, and the Religious Right's hysterical attempts to control the sexuality of others would be the panicked lashing-out of a dying lion. But the sexual obsession is a symptom of decay, not a cause, as religious moralists seem to think. Our conceptualization of the world is tottering, which leads to decadence. Religious conservatives spot this decadence and point to it as a sign of the end, which it surely is. But instead of toppling the crumbling edifice over and building anew, they seek to go back to an impossible naiveté, before evil old Darwin told us we descended from monkeys; before premarital sex was thought *not* to earn you an eternity of Hellfire; and before actors were allowed to blaspheme on TV by shouting the name of Jesus when trying to act surprised.

Running to the consolations of promiscuous sex is a reaction predicated on the inability to psychologically or spiritually assimilate the modern world. It's no coincidence that Griffin plays a Female Security Guard. What does a security guard do? The same thing a security blanket does. Protect us from harm. What does Griffin as Female Security Guard do? By engaging in sexual congress with Animal, offers protection.

Now, Griffin and Animal's sexual act is based on lust, and because Animal is a "rock star," we have to assume that what is being explored is the dynamic of female attraction towards the rock star, or more honestly, The Rock Star Personality, which can exist in many spheres outside the music industry.

This is love of the Bad Boy, which when projected onto celebrities also involves love of wealth, fame, prestige, and freedom. The sexuality of the Mother, who is actually performing the functions of procreation, is considered boring, tame, and unfulfilling. Passionate, sultry dalliances with Bad Boys is exciting, satisfying, and fulfilling—one may even get a chance to ride on the Bad Boy's motorcycle.

The clearest expression of this is in the Rock Star Groupie, which, after abortion, might be called the grosses expression of our drive to infertility and subconscious cultural death-wish. The film *The Banger Sisters*, which sanctifies the commoditized and dehumanized life of a Groupie, might be considered amongst the most rotten propagandistic pieces in favor of this sexuality ever made. The next contender would be the nefariously bad *The Girl Next Door*, which softens the reality of the porn industry and glorifies the myth of freedom through sexuality. It stars the infinitely untalented Elisha Cuthbert, who in interviews has said she enjoys transmitting herpes to unsuspecting sexual partners.

In the end, Animal is left to distract Kathy Griffin, allowing the others to achieve their goals. It is clear later that Animal has sexuall satisfied her. She says call me, he says "whatever." *Muppets From Space* thus tells us that in the community of avant-garde seekers and spiritual leaders of the future, there will be some unable to overcome their destructive addiction to sensuality. These people must be abandoned, cast off as so much dead weight, just as the entire project of "freedom through sexuality" must be. It should not be much trouble when we consider "libertine sexual obsession" under the illuminating light of Critical Theory: as just one more mode capitalistic civilization has of dehumanizing its members while making them believe they have been empowered.

These sensualists may rejoin the pack of bold spiritual innovators some time in the future, as Animal regroups with the other Muppets, but it will be necessary to do away with them for a period of time so they do not distract others from the goal at hand.

Similarly, after Gonzo's extraction from COVNET, Singer removes from its hiding place a super-advanced weapon, a ray-gun or energy blaster developed presumably to counter alien technology if we should ever be attacked. As the audience, we know Singer's reliance on the gun is as misguided as mankind's reliance on technology alone. The foe we face is not a technical challenge, or a problem amenable to the solution processes of science. Spiritual, psychological, social, and aesthetic techniques must be developed and consulted.

After rescuing Gonzo, the Muppet gang makes its way to Cape Doom for the final showdown with the alien race. There are already hundreds of people gathered there, anxious to welcome the alien visitors.

I'm quite certain nobody needs me to now point out the fact that Gonzo's problem, and thus mankind's, is an oppressive feeling of homelessness in the abstract sense. But both fire and oil drums make us think of energy, and mostly the consumption of energy. And the energy consumption we think of most is the burning of fossil fuels, primarily oil. The barrel is emptied of its contents, suggesting the oil has been used. This could be taken as a metaphor, suggesting that our reserves of the spiritual energy appropriate to the modern age have been all used up, and like oil the supply was finite.

Now that it's time for the development or discovery of a new spiritual energy, one for the next millennium, we find ourselves at a loss, and have reverted back to the use of fire. Meaning, we have reverted back to the level of our primitive ancestors. Just as the domination of fire meant for cavemen a technology-propelled leap into a new era, so shall our discovery of new means of energy. But we are out of the old energy, and none have taken its place, so we reach back in time and bring into today what should properly remain buried in the past—and by that I mean all the irrational forms of thinking, from believing in ghosts to tarot cards, Ouija boards, spirit-channeling, and astrology.

But why should Dawson's gang be roasting s'mores? S'mores are a favorite treat when camping out in the wilderness. Camping out in the wilderness is how we moderns get in tune with nature, how many of us rejuvenate ourselves. We get away from our urban or suburban surroundings and get out amongst the trees and flowers and rivers. But camping is conveniences, even if it's just manufactured pants and a buck-knife. You and I cannot go back to the wilderness, and it is not by taking steps backwards in our retreat from modernity that will cause us to stumble over our destiny. We can only stumble forward. A stumble backwards will be the end of humanity, and our death. As Einstein said, if there is a nuclear world war, then the world war after that will be fought with sticks and stones. Only a catastrophic event can jar us backwards into a real state of "noble savagery," and when we get there we will find that the primitive world was not all feasting and dancing around the fire giving praise to The Great Spirit. There was also a lot of dying and ignorance and suffering and disease. Yet that is the only state wherein we can authentically be "blissful primitives." *Dances With Wolves* may have gotten the Academy Award for Best Picture, but it was as much a fairly-tale as the universally panned *Waterworld*, which destroyed Kevin Costner's career. not living the life of Grizzly Adams. We bring along various modern

So by roasting s'mores we are to understand that to romanticize primitivism is a mere masturbatory exercise by hippies and potheads, and not a realistic or desirable plan of action. What is more, like a s'more, it may taste good but is hardly a nutritional meal, just as fantasies of escaping into the imaginary past are not particularly nutritive.

There is one more possible explanation of the *Dawson's Creek* insertion. My final conclusion is practically a mystical hypothesis, but we need not follow the argument that far in order to consider it amongst the list of plausible interpretations. This is the second time in *Space Muppets* that the Fourth Wall is broken, the first being the introduction of Hollywood Hulk Hogan. Now, I could easily assume that they broke the Fourth Wall this second time just to create narrative balance. I would probably even leave it at that if I possessed a mind less attuned to critical analysis. One cameo and one wall-breaking centers too much focus on the first third of the movie.

When considering a piece of dramatic art, one has to understand that both cameos and breakages of the Fourth Wall create audience "trauma." By being bluntly reminded of the fact that we are watching a film or play, we are also being asked to shift gears in our cognition. Suspension of disbelief, essential to the appreciation of most dramatic arts, becomes an impediment to enjoying the dramatic arts that tear the Fourth Wall down. But this also means that there will be a too-great concentration of cognitive energy around the scene or moment in which the Fourth Wall was actually broken.

Thus, if *Space Muppets* went on until the credits rolled without a second breaking of the Fourth Wall, the scene with Hulk Hogan would have stood out as utterly ridiculous and a symptom of bad or thoughtless movie-making. It would have left a bad taste in our mouths when we left the theater. But by sticking a "breakage" at the end of the first act, and then again at the beginning of the third and last act, balance comes into the film. It is hung, buoyed, or balanced, so to speak, on two points, like a coat hung on two posts when there are several empty knobs between the two supporting posts (and on either side).

But this use of two "posts," so to speak, makes the "posts" stand out apart from the general narrative in the film itself, just as we can see the outlines of the hanging-knobs pushing against the fabric of our coat. In other words, the two balance points in the film stand out as interruptions in the narrative of the film and also a jarring removal from the world of the film. Thus it seems they are intended to be considered apart from the film, and so we must think about what they mean in relation to one another when outside the context of the storyline.

But if my analysis of the Hulk Hogan cameo is correct, it was intended to plant the seeds of revolution in the mind of some child living in the dystopian future. It was to do this by creating a kind of cognitive dissonance by highlighting the gap between expectations the film has about its audience and the jarring effect these expectations have upon the future child's mind. Through this cognitive jarring he is to be freed from his mental conditioning by the mass media, the brainwashing and propaganda tool for a race of soulless machines who have enslaved the entire human race.

And this because an incomprehensible cameo leads him to the recognition that mass entertainment negates the very existence of the viewer, who passively consumes propaganda and never interacts with it as art. This child is then to lead a revolution against the machines, like John Connor in *The Terminator* or Neo in *The Matrix*. But then, having unlocked the secret to the first cameo, and then having experienced the effect it was intended to have very far off in the future when viewing the second cameo, would imply I have solved the riddle. I would therefore have to think that I myself was this Conner-like savior. In that case, the time for revolution would be now.

In quick summation of the final minutes of the film, the gathered crowd becomes awestruck when the UFO appears like fire in the sky, in the shape of a metallic egg. The egg of course represents birth and the very seed of life, a final example of a theme suggested throughout the movie. The birth referred to here is that of the rebirth of man into a new relationship to the cosmos. Probably having assumed that no aliens would arrive (as they never do at these kinds of gatherings), the people's jaws now hang slackly agape, in an anticipatory state not far removed from fear.

At the sign of the "space egg" Rizzo makes the Sign of the Cross (being an Italian stereotype, he is of course Catholic). Though many think that the existence of alien life should deal a significant blow to religious faith, it is rightly implied that a common reaction to living proof of alien civilizations will be a regressive reliance on older, fundamentally obsolete religious forms. If and when our notion of being the only intelligent life in the universe is so rudely disrupted, we will surely attempt to fit them into our own spiritual narratives, at least early on. It will take some time before we completely surrender to the massive paradigm shift involved in such a profound awakening.

Through Rizzo's gesture, we see that it is traditional religious forms being singled out as the womb of ignorant bliss to which we will attempt retreat. we know that astrology and ancient forms of "wisdom" are also suspect. When the egg lands the people crowd around. At first nothing happens, but then the egg unfolds into an enormous stage complete with fog-sprayers, colored lights, and pyrotechnics. They perform a funk number, and we are to be reminded of Parliament's "Mothership Connection" days, when they arrived on stage in a giant UFO wearing flamboyant space-ranger costumes.

A number of funk music classics have played throughout the film, and primarily compose the soundtrack. This association with Parliament and P-Funk is essential to the final moments of the film because funk music is mostly associated with party music, and while the Parliament lineup and stage antics may have been freakish and strange, the music was nevertheless all about having fun and dancing. In essence, the music familiarized one to the presence of the utterly bizarre and unknown. The album "Mothership Connection" itself combines themes of redemption with science fiction, drugs, and traditional slave spirituals. To fully explore the meaning of Parliament and funk in the film would require an exhaustive analysis of the music, and unfortunately for us this is not the appropriate forum for such an undertaking.

Gonzo learns from his alien kin that he was lost a long time ago, and that they've been roaming the galaxy ever since on a desperate quest to find him. There is no explanation for how or why he was lost. It is simply stated as a disagreeable fact. And just as there is no explanation for Gonzo being lost, there is similarly no explanation of how or why we humans are lost. The evolution of civilization could have proceed along myriad courses, and we have no true explanations of why we find ourselves today in such existentially perilous circumstances.

The fractured psyche we exhibit is a symptom of social decay, and a sense of being lost is probably the most commonly felt malaise, at least among the spiritually sensitive among us. The consciousness with which we have been saddled was always prone to feelings of dislocation, and indeed must be the source of our religious yearning, especially as so many religions, regardless of how they've been coopted by state powers, began as religious wisdom from the mouths of those who didn't feel a sense of belonging to the societies in which they lived.

Gonzo is shot from the cannon, as he refused to do for the Bar Mitvah. He is now a Superman. But is he a NIetzshcean Overman?

While the impromptu party rages, Singer stumbles through the crowd, ray-gun at the ready, and attempts to fire it on the funk-playing aliens. But Bobo the Bear has removed the power-cell so that the gun does not fire. While trying to retrieve the cell, Singer stumbles about like a fool, demonstrating a small knack for pratfalls and slapstick physical comedy. This scene suggests that with the end of the Cold War (Bobo the Bear is a Russian stand-in, remember), America's continuing focus on technological advancements to approach the problems of today, and those on the horizon, is becoming every day more absurd.

Take for example the bumbling President Bush's early insistence on the development of a Reaganesque nuclear shield, which no serious thinker, political or scientific, considered a feasible idea or worthwhile use of government coffers. This after 9/11 demonstrated that our most pressing security concern wasn't stopping nuclear weapons, but rather, rooting out the enemies in our midst. But even more pressing in the long term is not our national security, but our national identity. Ambivalence about our nature, character, and destiny as a people has crept into our psyche, and uniting Americans under one banner has only become more difficult, as popular media continues to fragment into smaller and more niche chunks.

It may appear impossible, in these days, to launch a paradigm that influences each and every one of us. Ideologies no longer seem monolithic to us, or overarching. However, the irony of our age—that the closer we are tied in with social media and communications technology—the further we drift from one another, may not even be an irony. For this sense of distance may not reflect a real distance, and we may be a more malleable collective than any era in history has known. If so, we will have to rely on those societal institutions which have the greatest degree of influence on our individual and social psychology, and pray the members of these institutions recognize the need our nation has for a full-tilt paradigm shift.

Singer's greatest fear is being laughed at, and as he trips and stumbles nobody can suppress their hearty chuckles. This buffoonery makes him vulnerable, and thus exposes him to possibilities of change. We find that being laughed at is not he worst thing that can happen to us.

Because he makes the alien race laugh so hard, they decide to make Singer Earth's ambassador to their home planet. A role which he cautiously, but nevertheless enthusiastically, accepts. It seems that Singer, like Gonzo, has been looking for a home, and merely relied on aggressive tactics directed outwardly while Gonzo became withdrawn and resigned. They rename Singer as Zongo, both to indicate his role as doppelganger to Gonzo, and to baptize him into a new level of cosmic awareness. One in which the universe is seen as something far more magical and beautiful than the narrow mindset which posits the natural world as a threat.

In the end Gonzo stays on Earth, having realized he does have a home here, and he finds his home in the friends and loved ones who surround him.

In a way, the ending of the film is both a cop-out and expressive of a very profound truth. Throughout all of history and literature, recognizing one's fellow man as the remedy to cosmic angst has been preached. In our own canonical arts, Melville's *Moby Dick*, after many intense revelations about the nature of life and the universe, concludes that the one bulwark we have against succumbing to despair is the companionship of our fellows. This is the conclusion which tends to mirror what is best in humanism. However, it is not the only solution conceivable.

For example, in *2001: A Space Odyssey*, Kubrick posits a shift upward in mankind's actual state of consciousness, similar in kind to the shift which took place from unconscious simian to conscious human. Kubrick's salvation and rescue from modernity entails a change so radical in degree that our state of personal consciousness in that future stage would, in relation to our contemporary one, resemble the comparison of our consciousness level to that of an ape's. There is no real social element to Kubrick's "overcoming" of the old self, it is entirely personal and hoisted on the individual, although as a human phenomenon it will of necessity entail social ramifications. Another non-social solution to the dilemma is represented in the life of the mystic, secular or otherwise. Sarte said, "Hell is other people," and Nietzsche would have considered finding one's redemption in other people a plebian move appropriate only to those with a hypertrophied herd instinct.

In the end Gonzo is a spirit of mediocre rank. This is not intended as an insult; only as description. Most of us belong to "the multitude," and being undistinguished in that way, might just find our salvation in the love, laughter, and joy we gain in the company of other human beings. This is the kind of soul for whom friends and family sate the hunger for meaning.

But there are those of us in this world who try to look beyond our friends and family for spiritual fulfillment. We are the religious ones.

It is really the illustration of Irony that in America, those who most trumpet the importance of family are also the most religious and God-fearing. Believing in a God who surpasses all Earthly things in importance by logical necessity diminishes the meaning of family. What is family in comparison to the Almighty? Necessarily a trifle, and this in all seriousness. Most of us really do probably love our family more than God, but to admit that would be blasphemy.

This is probably why religious people tout God and Family as being more or less interlinked. Their loyalty and love is divided, between that which they themselves created, did in fact issue from their own loins, and that which they were created by. This is why Christianity, and Western religion, have such difficulty entering the new world. Judeo-Christianity is nothing more, really, than a generational conflict, with ourselves in the middle. Both child and parent, we must decide who adore more, our parent or are children. This observation alone makes traditional religion worthy of a suspicious eye.

It must be said that though *Muppets From Space*'s humanistic conclusions are sound, they may not represent the solutions necessary to spirits of rarer sensitivity. There will always be those who plow into the frontiers of religious experience, and find that simply surrendering to the social instinct never garners the solutions they most ardently seek. Most of our kind's religious geniuses were acquainted with solitude. Though their practices and conclusions were taken up by disciples for whom they made sense, we can conclude that most religious epiphanies were first and foremost personal matters.

The atheist, who really shoulders the responsibility for leading us into the next spiritual phase, can easily grow weary. He knows that his push towards mystical experience can but lead him to a mirror, whence he must pull awakening from his own reflection. The religious thinker has never been so alone as in our time, and being without god or gods, is by accident of his birth damned to a solitude more daunting than has ever been known. But if he perseveres and is not crushed by his solitude, it is to his ramble that we will march into the unfolding future.

In my darkest hours, inky as ebony, I come to suspect that in the final analysis all *Muppets From Space* really accomplished—and all its creators intended of it—was to accommodate children to the Unknown. It pains the film analyst to entertain the possibility that this film's most urgent message was to promote the painfully banal pipe dream that familiarity with the Unknown makes it less frightening. If in our day and age we don't fear the Known in equal measure to the Unknown, we either aren't paying attention or have numbed ourselves to the general disagreeability of life, and the deeply nihilistic picture modern science paints for us.

What is Known, when properly digested, should fill us with despair. After such profound buildup, if this film's flat finale was the one really and truly aimed at, we will have to relegate this brilliant work of art to the rubbish pile. That selfsame heap where we cast all those pretty truths we're told as children, but which through worldly experience we find to be false and hollow as an old stump.

It's even possible that this glorious film was conceived *merely* to socialize youth to the acceptance of ethnicities and nationalities different from our own, and of course those unjustly shunned souls, the handicapped. It is thought by many in pedagogical fields that the seeds of racism and prejudice are to be found in our natural fear of the unknown, especially the so-called Other. If so it may be in spite of the film's narrow, limited, and preachy perspective of "tolerance for what is different," that we have before us a great film, one that surpasses all of the highest expectations of what a movie is capable of achieving.

Sometimes great art is accidental. And though "morally instructive" art undermines its own existence as art, individuals always reflect at some deep level the zeitgeist of the age, which in our case is the basic need to ward off existential frights of bloodcurdling reality with cheerful and congenial entertainments. And though we accept that creating a generation of young people whose fear of the Other is minimized is a worthwhile undertaking, it is only by accepting the Known as what is truly to be feared, that we can assimilate and overcome the dire implications of knowledge. Mere advocacy for preferred ethical stances ignores what are more fundamentally the woes of our age.

As for myself, I prefer to believe the good people behind the film wrote it so as to address the problems of Modernity, despite an ending that appeared to greatly diminish the theme. As such, *Muppets From Space* will stand among the most insightful depictions of our melancholic age. It will be pertinent until some unknown day far in the future, when we will have adopted a new life-affirming ideology that manages both to incorporate our existential truth and uplift our spirits.

Should that Golden Age arrive, *Muppets From Space* will still be invaluable as a cultural product of singular relevance, and ever afterward as an artwork instructive of humanity's "dark night of the soul." Like Gonzo in the introductory dream sequence, we have no Noah's Ark to save us from our eventual annihilation. However, it is my sincerest hope that filling all our lives are those types of people who make life itself beautiful and worth living. Until there is a suitable spirituality for mankind's next phase of existence, we are yet able to look to each another for our cheerfulness, and remain optimistic in the face of our collective calamity.

We are, all of us, Gonzo.

What is sacred and eternal in *Muppets From Space* is our common human experience as co-passengers on the frightening carnival ride of contemporary existence, hand in hand, faces turned upward at the vast indifferent cosmos stretching out for untold eons before our eyes. In brief, if the Muppets in this film advocate any salvation, it is the salvation we find in universal brotherhood and comradeship

If this seems altogether too ambitious a theme for a Muppet movie, I encourage you to revisit the film, this time seeking out the clues that will aid you in unpacking this work of art. As adventurers in film theory, we by no means impose our own interpretations on a work, forcing it to awkwardly justify wayward musings. Rather, we let the work speak for itself. But to really hear a work such as *Muppets From Space*, one must have the ears for it. Every line, every detail, every plot point, opens up a veritable web-work of new ideas and opportunities for analysis. The film is an infinite nesting doll of associations, as are all the very best creative products that sprout forth from the human imagination.

Any serious theorist has experienced the skeptical naysayer who doubts what they've discovered in a work of art. Rest assured, these people simply do not have the vision, or are denying the hard reality that nothing we consume, no cultural product, is innocuous. There is always a message, implicit or explicit, conscious or subconscious. Nothing we experience is innocuous; everything that exists is integrated in the web of existence. As such, it cannot help but comment on existence. There is really nothing in life that is a mere "diversion." But again, one must have the eyes for it. But first of all, one must have the will for it. The will to actually step back and attempt to see the world for what it is. And what is, for all its joys and perks and moments of life-affirming exhilaration, is a slog through a swamp of suffering and uncertainty.

Why the music is funk music.

If I may be excused a moment of gentle nationalism and patriotism; that this product is American-made, and a quintessential product of our unconscious American mythos—echoing the themes and concerns of our Great Epic *Moby Dick*—makes me as an American very proud. As the obscurantism, resentment, and spiritual decadence of continental Europe drives those old Occidental civilizations deeper down into the garbage compactor of historical irrelevance; and as fundamentalist Islam threatens to plunge the world into what could conceivably be the darkest age ever known to all mankind, it is up to we Americans, with our effete but otherwise lovable sibling to the North, Canada; and our perpetually drunk but magnanimous cousins to the South, the rambunctious Australians; and our beloved English-speaking British and Irish kin, who practically alone carry the torch of masculinity in Europe—it is up to us to carry forward into the future the torch of Western Civilization. *Muppets From Space*, by encouraging the youth of today to share good laughs with good friends, offers the upcoming generations a spiritual toolkit from which they can draw strength whenever the terrors of the dark void seem too heavy to be borne aloft. And adults too may find in this wonderwork a few special treasures and nuggets of spiritual wisdom—specifically, the totems and charms that form the bulwark of our spiritual resistance to metaphysical despair. If our existential crisis is the world, and we are Atlas crumbling under the burden, *Muppets From Space* is a brief respite from our labors, and perhaps a source of new strength, a map to new wells of inexhaustible endurance.

It is for these reasons that if somebody wants to really feel something, and not only enjoy an abstract intellectualization of a feeling, give him *Muppets From Space* over any Ingmar Bergman or Bruno Dumont film. And all this is not to say that the writing or conceptions in *Muppets From Space* are Shakespearean in their grandeur—for such would be the height of folly. Rather, it is to say this: When a filmmaker is a spirit of mediocre rank, he often chooses to overreach himself, whether it is to illustrate abstract points which he does not fully understand, or by making ham-fisted, knee-jerk social commentary from half-baked points-of-view he hasn't the mental prowess to think through to their logical conclusions. If Shakespeare is the epitome,

With European filmmaking it is different. When we watch an intellectual or artistic European film, we catch on the breeze what seems to be the dying breath of an old man, a civilization too worn out to produce anything but bile and hatred against the still-buoyant and joyful beings who pulse with energy and life; a people too spiritually decayed and corrupt to value itself as anything other than the world's hysterical conscience, in matters as diverse as global climate change, human rights and, above all, aesthetics.

Conversely, there is a brighter, healthier instinct; one more cheerful, knowing, and abundant with the stuff of life. This leads a mediocre filmmaker to the decision that he must not contend and try to match in the arts what history's greatest philosophers have stated, so instead makes a picture whose glorious and golden effusions pour out directly from the human breast.

st in the history of thought.

What we have in *Muppets From Space* is an expression of humanity's compromise with the godless and horrifying cosmos. Until certainty about our role in the universe is confirmed and established, we humans must encourage and maintain a humorous and light-hearted disposition, if only because this is the last weapon civilized humanity has against a foreboding and forbidden nihilism. That, and the gift of human sociability and fraternity, will keep us unafraid as we walk through the shadowy valley. Perhaps this is only an American aesthetic and philosophical device, one of our great motifs and grand narratives, as our Great American Epic, *Moby Dick*, dealt with similar matters and arrived at similar conclusions. There is of course another approach to the horrible cosmos, the Lovecraftian one, in which humanity is considered an isolated island of sanity in a universe that has practically become a declared enemy to humankind. For my money, and perhaps merely because it better suits my cheerful countenance, I prefer the *Moby Dickian/Muppets From Spacian* response, which is a faith that laughter is our only defense against the howling abyss of space, and friendship our only lifeboat in the unknown, heartless sea.

Some peripheral but no less evocative reasons for casting Tambor as Singer may be noted. Firstly, his role in the cancelled but critically acclaimed television program *Arrested Development*. In the show he plays a materially successful Jew alienated from his family and his religious tradition, George

Bluth. Thus he is symbolic of the general malaise of the contemporary bourgeoisie. The title *Arrested Development* also echoes the arrested *spiritual* development of Gonzo.

Also, Tambor starred in the Jim Carrey remake of *The Grinch Who Stole Christmas*, a tale about an irate and resentful Jewish troll who attempts to destroy the Christ-mythos and avenge the usurpation of the Hebrew Bible. In essence, Seuss's classic is a defensive tale wielded against the onslaught of embittered Jewish atheism against the fundamental value systems that serve as the bedrock of Christendom. This onslaught has its source in such luminaries as Freud; Marx; Marvin Harris; Jake Gyllenhaal (the gay cowboy who prefers his sodomy rough, dry, and in a tent after camping for three weeks); and the painfully unfunny and presumably unintelligent Ashkenazi, Sarah Silverman.

Thus in a conceptual turnabout, Jim Carrey, raised French-Canadian Catholic and known to affiliate occasionally with Protestant denominations, represents the resentful Jewish intellectual destruction of Christianity, and even breathes life into the theory Judaism is itself a reactive theology based on ethnic nationalism. This while Tambor's function in the film is to represent Christianity gone astray, and to accuse it of having become selfish, materialistic, hateful, shallow, bigoted and spiritually unsatisfying.

Thus Tambor offers a critique of the usurpation of Christianity by Capitalism in form, and Consumerism in content; and Carrey exposes hatred of Christianity as blindness to its importance as a cultural phenomena removed from its theological underpinnings. This attempt destroys the validity of both creeds, and thus the foundations of Judeo-Christian civilization. But in the world of the film we are rescued from nihilism by the final scene's endorsement of universal fraternity. And in the world of reality, we are said to be saved from nihilism by the very act of consuming entertainment products. This consumption might very well be one of our modern sacraments; our Eucharist in a way, if by Eucharist we mean mindful commemoration of the mechanics by which we receive salvation.

For some reason, the primary cast from the television show *Dawson's Creek* are there, roasting s'mores over a fire burning in a steel oil drum. Some of the Muppets stop and talk to them. Once again, I stumble when it comes to analyzing this cameo, but I hesitate no doubts that the fault is purely my own. Perhaps I lack the imagination, but probably I just lack familiarity. Though aware of the show's existence, I have never seen an episode of *Dawson's Creek*, nor do I know what it said about America in the late 90's and early 2000's.

Firstly, I was never the kind to watch teen dramas on television, even while in my teens. I found them insipid and pandering. But mostly I hated the insult they presented to my intelligence. And though I am aware there was a large college audience for the program, by the time I was twenty years old I had pretty much passed out of my television-watching phase. I was living with a woman, working full time, and going to school full time. I definitely did not have time for any of adolescent Dawson's pusillanimous, melodramatic bullshit.

That said, after researching the program on Wikipedia, I have a vague sense of what the show was up to thematically. Basically *Dawson's Creek* was a straight-faced teen weeper. It dealt somberly with "issues" like homosexuality, sex, drugs, and I'm sure it dealt with racism because you can't have your drama taken seriously if it doesn't deal "intelligently" with racism. Basically, it was the perfect show for an effeminate, emotionally pampered generation coming of age in the aftermath of Nirvana, Pearl Jam, and that one pussy-ass band that sings about runaway trains or two kids fighting in a schoolyard or some shit—the lead singer used to date Claire Daines or Winona Ryder. I always think their name is Collective Soul, but then I remember no, it was another band that sucked, but they also had the word soul in their name, and all of a sudden it dons on me like a flash and I remember that their name is—yes!—*Soul Asylum!*

Maybe because *Dawson's Creek* supposedly dealt with real "issues," and issues teens really care about, we're supposed to recognize that the cosmological, existential, and spiritual issues of our day are important to today's youth, and we cannot characterize them as a mere gang of "slackers." You know, like in that film fags really seemed to enjoy, *Reality Bites*. In such a film we see that the young, sensitive slacker/poet/bohemian/philosopher is really the truest human being seeking out a truer world, and that's why he values authenticity so very much. He can't stand any of that yuppie or bourgeois materialism—he wants to play rock and folk songs and start a revolution in the coffee shops, and make the world a place were presidents are poets and poets are presidents.

Maybe we're supposed to see that the *Dawson's Creek* Generation's angst and teenage malaise is a reaction to adult society's failure in addressing the existential crises of our time, and not a product of hormones, puberty, or the pangs which accompany a growing sense of self-dependence and personal autonomy. What say you?

Or maybe the reference to *Dawson's Creek* is a magician's sleight-of-hand, and we are really supposed to pay attention to what they are doing in the scene. And what are they doing? They are cooking s'mores over a fire built in an oil drum. A fire built in an oil drum can conjure up several associations. Firstly, it makes us think of homelessness. The archetypal scene for the fire in the oil drum is that of a group of ragged homeless people grouped around one trying to warm their hands. Obviously homelessness is the state of not having a home, and a home can be both physical and abstract.

www.ingramcontent.com/pod-product-compliance
Lightning Source LLC
Chambersburg PA
CBHW071021240526
45469CB00006BD/2027